THE AUTHOR

MANEATERS AND MARAUDERS

MANEATERS AND MARAUDERS

by

JOHN TAYLOR

("Pondoro")

author of
Pondoro: Last of the Ivory-Hunters, etc.

Safari Press

Taylor, John

Safari Press Inc.
2005, Long Beach, California

ISBN 1-57157-311-9

Library of Congress Catalog Card Number: 2004096242

10 9 8 7 6 5 4 3 2

Printed in the USA

Readers wishing to receive the Safari Press catalog, featuring many fine books on big-game hunting, wingshooting, and sporting firearms, should write to Safari Press Inc., P.O. Box 3095, Long Beach, CA 90803, USA. Tel: (714) 894-9080 or visit our Web site at www.safaripress.com.

To

ALY NDEMANGA

and

the many other staunch, faithful friends,
servants and companions who have
accompanied me throughout the many
years of my African wanderings, and
without whose ever-willing help I could
not have succeeded in my endeavours.

Author's Note

The Author adheres to the hunter's pre-
ference for the singular form where
game animals are concerned (lion, elephant, buffalo, etc.); non-game animals
(crocodiles, baboons, etc.) are given the
customary plurals.

CONTENTS

LIST OF ILLUSTRATIONS

Foreword

Since, from its very subject matter, it is inevitable that a considerable amount of killing is described in the following pages, it has been deemed desirable to say something about it in a Foreword and offer an explanation which even the less liberal-minded may feel is a justification. After all, there are few who would not feel justified in killing, or having someone else kill, a mad dog, especially if that animal were endangering their children. The same people would without doubt complain bitterly if homicidal maniacs were permitted to roam at large and were not put out of the way. That being so, there does not appear to be any very good reason for special pleading in the case of a professional hunter who spends much of his time hunting and shooting maneating lion, leopard or crocs.

The position is rather different, however, whenever elephant and buffalo are mentioned. Those who have not lived in, and actually seen, the devastation caused by herds of these great beasts can be excused for believing that accounts of the damage they do must be exaggerated. I only wish it were so! I can think of few more ghastly sights than that of little children slowly starving: the bones of their arms and legs almost sticking through the skin: their ribs like barrel-hoops above tummies grotesquely distended from eating grass and leaves and roots: while their great eyes are sunk far back in deep hollows, and know that all this has been caused by the depredations of either elephant or buffalo, or both. But I have seen all this; not just once or twice, but all too often. Sometimes what we see are the visible effects of prolonged malnutrition which first take the form of sloughing ulcers on the legs which just will not heal but get gradually larger and larger. If animals are the cause of these conditions, then those animals must be restrained from continuing their depredations. The only known method of restraining them is by shooting a certain number out of each herd or party whenever they come raiding the food crops.

The British do so to a greater or lesser extent in those of their territories wherein elephant are numerous. They call it the "Elephant Control Scheme"; vast tracks of country are declared elephant reserves, after any natives who were previously living there have been removed and given land elsewhere upon which to build new homes. Any elephant that come out of the reserve to raid the crops of the people living outside are shot by an army of well-trained and well-armed native hunters who are paid a monthly salary by the government and supervised by whites. Elephant are very intelligent and quickly learn their lesson. However, it will readily be understood that such an organisation needs considerable capital to start with. Later the scheme will make a handsome profit for government which claims all ivory shot under Control operations by its hunters.

Unfortunately, in the days of which I mainly write, the Portuguese were poor and were quite unable to find the necessary funds with which to commence a similar Control Scheme. The result was that elephant continued to raid the unfortunate natives' food crops; and, in addition to the large numbers of elephant which swarmed throughout Portuguese territory, there came vastly increased numbers of invaders from the surrounding British territories: Tanganyika, Northern Rhodesia, etc. There had always been a certain number of seasonal visitors across the territorial frontiers; but those were now considerably augmented by others which soon found out that in the Portuguese territory they could still raid the maize and millet they loved with little or no interference.

During the 1920's there were a considerable number of ivory hunters in Portuguese East; but they were concerned solely with shooting as much ivory as they could in the shortest possible time. They had no concern whatsoever with the welfare of the local natives: all they cared about was getting as many porters as they could whenever they needed them and paying them the absolute minimum wage. During the world slump which reached Africa about 1929 or '30, the price of ivory dropped to next to nothing, and all those men quit hunting for it. This meant that the elephant, not being interferred with to anything like the same extent, recommenced breeding at their normal rate. And this in turn meant that things got worse and worse for the local natives.

Throughout all that time I think I can have been the only hunter who cared even slightly about the natives: at any rate, I did not hear of a single other who would go a mile out of his way to shoot a maneater, much less spend weeks or months hunting and shooting them in some area where they had been creating a positive reign of terror. There was no profit to be made out of maneaters, and those concerned solely in hunting for profit were not interested in the misfortunes of the native population. But I was not primarily concerned with profits: just so long as I could pay my way and keep my spare ammunition bag well-filled I was content. I looked upon the African as my friend and was always ready and willing to help him. The natives knew that and therefore did not hesitate to send for me whenever they were being troubled by marauders or maneaters. But Portuguese East Africa is an immense piece of country and I could not be in more than one place at a time. My hunting was mainly up and down along the Zambezi valley; in Portuguese Angoniland; and up in the East Nyasa province, south of the Rovuma, which forms the boundary of Portuguese East Africa (P.E.A.) and Tanganyika. Since throughout the 'twenties and early 'thirties I had no motor transport, but had to walk except when I was canoeing, travelling from one end of my "district" to the other was a lengthy business. Later, when I was able to get myself a car of sorts, things improved considerably—at least, they did after roads had been built throughout; though that didn't really come until after I got back from the second World War. Up to then there had slowly come roads of a kind which were passable only for a few months during the dry season.

I received no payment for my work in stopping the marauders. I was not a wealthy man. My rifles were my sole means of livelihood, and, if I were to continue to help the Africans, I had to do something to enable me to keep going. I recouped my expenses by keeping any ivory I managed to shoot when driving away marauders; and when there was not sufficient then I had to make sorties amongst well-tusked elephant, whether or not they had been raiding food crops.

The Portuguese authorities fully appreciated the work I was doing. They realised that it was work they should have been doing themselves, if they could have afforded it; and they showed their appreciation by granting me an unrestricted permit every year. Up to the outbreak of World War II, no other such permit was granted to anyone, not even to their own nationals. Had I been restricted, or been forced to pay for permits, I could not have carried on.

So, special pleading or not, I would ask you to bear the above facts in mind as you read on.

JOHN TAYLOR,
P.E.A.

The Benga Maneaters

I USED to have a small trading store at Benga on the Revugwi not far from its confluence with the Zambezi, and had given the native who ran it for me an interest in the business so as to keep him on his toes. I had been coming up the Zambezi and turned into the mouth of the Revugwi, paddling along to the store which was built close to the bank. It was very hot and I chose to sleep in the open rather than in the store. My men were as usual sleeping close by. My storekeeper had tried to dissuade us from sleeping in the open because the area has always been known as a bad one for maneaters, although sometimes the local inhabitants would be free from them for a year or two. At this time, however, it was known that there were at least three potential maneaters around— probably a male and two females. They usually appeared together, though occasionally the brute was solitary. My store- keeper told me that three or four times during the past ten days or so a lion had been seen stalking some woman during the late evening when she was returning from drawing water, and that once or twice the animal's two companions had been seen watching. Moreover, the pug marks of three lion were to be seen along each and every path throughout the district and not only in the vicinity, but right in the centre, of the many kraals (villages) scattered about in this thickly-populated area. Although so far they had contented themselves with killing the villagers' pigs and goats, it was quite obvious that it was only a matter of time before they started man-killing.

It's a strange thing how maneaters continually appear in

the same districts throughout Eastern Africa. There are several areas known to me which are seldom free from this scourge. Time and again I have shot them out, but sooner or later there would come another S O S from the unfortunate people to the effect that a fresh reign of terror had commenced. This has been happening off and on, and fairly continuously, throughout the thirty-five years or more that I have been wandering about Eastern and Central Africa. At least three of these bad areas were referred to by Livingstone in one of his books, and he mentioned the dreadful sufferings of the natives from the depredations of maneating lions. Those areas are just as bad today. But why these particular areas should be so affected is a question I have never heard satisfactorily answered. Although I have studied the problem intensively right there on the spot, I have no answer either.

The suggestion usually put forward is that the local inhabitants have killed off all the game, but this is not an acceptable explanation. In the first place most, though not all, of these districts consist of dry thorn-bush which never holds much in the way of game, though there may be plenty of game not so very far away in more suitable country; then, secondly, some of these bad areas contain quite a respectable amount of the lions' normal prey; and, finally, no native methods of hunting would ever wipe out Africa's immense game population. Before the advent of the white man, Africa, from the Sudan to the Cape, was literally teeming with game—yet the natives had been there for centuries. It seems absurd to suggest that they have succeeded in little more than half a century in doing what they had signally failed to do throughout all those preceeding centuries. It is quite possible that in those districts where the natives are permitted to own muzzle-loaders they have greatly reduced the game population of recent years— shooting all they can while the going is good, in case some new law or regulation is brought in dispossessing them of their precious old gas-pipes. But they had no such weapons in Livingstone's day; and the natives only have them in one or two places today.

Nor certainly is the answer that these lion have been wounded and lost by inexperienced sportsmen. In most of those districts I was the only hunter, and I only entered the area in answer to an appeal for help. Neither can the explanation be that the lion are old and unable to catch the alert game; many of these brutes are in their prime and have more or less well-grown cubs with them. The problem seems to be insoluble. Yet Man is not the natural prey of any animal and, as I have often had occasion to state, the ordinary "hunting" lion will not interfere unless he is interfered with. I have had ample proof of that in my own experience.

But to return to Benga:

The night was so hot that after they had cooked their food even my Africans didn't want a fire and allowed it to die down. They were sleeping in a circle around the ashes of the fire, the nearest of them only a few feet away from my bed, the foot of which was some ten or twelve feet away from the road. My little cook-boy, whom I called Friday, did not for some reason join the circle but spread his sleeping mat between the foot of my bed and the road and lay down there all by himself.

Having had much experience in maneater country I had long trained myself to sleep with one eye and one ear open; moreover, there is an inner intuition which one can develop and which will always warn one of imminent danger either by day or by night. I had long learnt to trust implicitly in this "sixth sense", and had never known it to let me down.

The sky was cloudless, but there was no moon. Somewhere around midnight I partially awoke and saw little Friday get

B

up, pick up his sleeping mat by one corner and, dragging it behind him, walk drowsily over to the sleeping circle, drop the mat between two of the sleepers, lie down on it, kick his sheet over himself, and drop instantly asleep again. It looked almost as though he had been less than half-awake, almost sleep-walking in fact. The following morning he had but the vaguest recollection of shifting during the night and could give no reason for doing so. I really only saw him out of the corner of my eye since I was only partly awake, and, since I had not felt any premonition of danger, I did not bother to look around. Yet next morning we found the fresh pug mark of a lion within but a very few inches of where little Friday's head had been. Furthermore, there were the pug marks of two other lion on the sandy surface of the road a few yards away. Evidently the other two had stood there watching the one that approached us. But it was impossible to say at what hour of the night all this had taken place.

Had that lion sneaked up on the sleeping youngster and then for some inexplicable reason decided not to interfere with him? Or had he approached later after Friday had joined his companions, and was it merely coincidence that he had stopped just where the lad had been sleeping? Had that same inner intuition warned the boy subconsciously so that, still more or less asleep, he had changed his position shortly before the lion arrived?

Personally, I should be inclined to favour the last explanation. I find it difficult to believe that the lion would have approached so close as to be actually standing right over a sleeper merely out of curiosity.

Then why didn't he attack? Supposing, as we must, that Friday had already joined his companions when the lion arrived, then why didn't the lion pounce on me? His pug mark was only six feet from the foot of my bed, yet, as I have already mentioned, I experienced no trace of that inner warning. I would not have expected to have had if these had been ordinary "hunting" lions—I have many times had such approach very close at night when I was sleeping, as the lions' spoor clearly showed next morning, but because their approach had been merely out of curiosity I was in no danger.

But these were not ordinary lion who came to the camp at Benga. I take it that they had been working up sufficient courage during the past few weeks to overcome their natural instinctive fear of man, and had every intention of becoming maneaters. Ordinary lion seldom wander around by day, and most certainly do not stalk human beings, especially during daylight, as these beasts had been known to do—and as they did only the following morning. And to do so at 10 o'clock in the morning in such a district showed that they must have been very hungry and could not have fed the previous night, possibly not for several nights. It is quite apparent to me that they must have needed just that one extra night's hunger to start them off on their maneating career. Otherwise, judging by previous and subsequent experience, I would unquestionably have received my customary warning. Had little Friday not been subconsciously warned and compelled to shift his position, he would almost certainly have been taken. The temptation would have proved irresistable to that lion.

Looking back now over the past I am more firmly convinced than ever that nothing happens by "chance". Little Friday was with me for some nine or ten years; and during that period had what would usually be considered three very narrow escapes from maneaters—this one was the second. His first occurred some years previously when I was hunting in a certain remote and lonely valley. As usual when it's not raining or threatening rain, we were all sleeping in the open and had allowed the fire to die down. There were always lion roaring there because game abounded; but we did not take any notice of them as they had plenty to eat and never became a nuisance.

Again on this occasion I partially awakened during the night and saw Friday get up and go out into the surrounding forest to relieve a call of nature. I then saw him return and try to persuade his sleeping companion to come and throw stones at a hyena he had heard close-by. As his pal was too drowsy to be bothered, Friday lay down again beside him and went back to sleep. But it wasn't a hyena he had heard, as we found next morning: a lion had been approaching and had halted when only a very few yards away. Yet he hadn't grabbed the lad when he was squatting there, nor when, having finished his business, he got up and sauntered back to the camp.

An ordinary hunting lion might well have merely stood there and watched; but this was a very old and mangy lioness which soon after grabbed a stranger from the sleeping circle lying around the glowing embers of the fire. The victim was a man who had come over the border to visit us. I managed to get him back from the would-be maneater, which was shot the following night after breaking into a hut and killing an aged woman and two children. But why didn't the lioness kill my boy when he was squatting there with his back towards her? I have no explanation to offer. The lioness made her attack on the camp about half an hour later.

The following morning around 10 o'clock there was a great hullabaloo over the rise immediately in front of the camp. I knew there were several kraals there, and the commotion could only mean that there an attack by lion was in progress. I grabbed my rifle and bandolier of ammunition, and ran up the hill towards where I could hear the women shouting. Before I reached the top a man appeared on the crest and shouted to me that three lion had attacked a woman up there, and even now were eating a hog they had killed in the village. This certainly indicated great hunger. Sun-up and sun-down are the maneater's favourite hours for hunting; otherwise he mostly kills at night.

I ceased hurrying up the hill. It wasn't a very high one; but I don't like hills, and when possibly some quick shooting may be called for, I don't like arriving on the scene short of breath. Besides, I knew that if the lions were actually eating a hog, they wouldn't be leaving just yet.

When I reached the crest the man who had called down was waiting and told me all he knew. It appeared that a woman of the village had placed a reed mat down on the ground, just on the outskirts of the kraal. On the mat she had spread a basket or two of grain she had washed and was about to grind into meal. When she thought the grain must be dry enough she went out to collect it. Putting the two baskets one on top of the other on her head, she had then rolled up the reed mat and thrown it carelessly over her shoulder as she turned around to retrace her steps to the kraal. But something had made her glance over her back, and there she saw two lion standing looking at her and a third creeping up close behind her. She gave a scream, dropped the mat behind her, grabbed at the baskets on her head, and ran for her life. Fortunately for her, the lion sprang on the fallen mat and tried to "kill" it, which gave the woman time to reach the comparative safety of the kraal. All this had taken place within about ten paces of the huts. As there were several men and women in the kraal, the lion did not venture to face them in broad daylight, so contented themselves with killing a hog which happened to pass at that moment. They had carried it a short distance away and were eating it when I arrived.

I found a dense black throng of spectators drawn up in semi-circular formation, determined to have ringside seats at this circus. They would not have been so eager to close in to feeding lion out in the bush; but here, so close to their homes and in broad day, they could not imagine they were in any danger. I knew I should have an almost impossible job to shoo them away; but I also knew they would keep their distance when told to do so. True, that distance wasn't very great—certainly not more than from twenty to twenty-five yards from where they eagerly pointed out the three lion to me; but I felt satisfied that they would not come in any closer and interfere with my line of fire, nor would they attempt to interfere with the lion.

But what I did not like to see was the inevitable half-breed with his old shotgun. I have many good friends amongst the half-breeds, and it must not be imagined that I am disparaging men of mixed blood in general; but unfortunately I have time and again had one of them appear on the scene just when I was about to take a shot at some maneater. Almost invariably they have made a mess of things. They WILL try and show off before the natives and impress upon them that they are just as brave and as competent as the white man, as, of course, in many cases they are. The trouble is that they are seldom suitably armed, and even when they are they are liable to become excited and shoot wildly without taking care to place their shots accurately in a vital spot; the inevitable result is a wounded and potentially dangerous beast or two to follow up. As the following-up is left to me, I find this kind of interference can be infuriating.

I signed to the big semi-circle of natives not to attempt to edge in any closer and waved the half-breed back. He glowered at me, but very reluctantly drew away until he was amongst the natives. However, I knew very well that as soon as I closed in he would come forward again, but I hoped to get in at least two shots before he got busy with that old shotgun of his.

It is difficult to contact these maneaters in the continuous thorn-scrub in which they mostly live, and one naturally wants to wipe out each and every member of a party when at last one gets the chance. This seemed as though it might be one of those rare chances one dreams about—if it hadn't been for the fellow with the gun. I knew he would let rip after my first or second shot, and thereby almost certainly lose me a shot at the third maneater. However, there was nothing I could do about it now. To have gone up to him and taken the gun from him would only have resulted in an argument, and an argument was obviously undesirable with the three lion only a short twenty yards away. The native hogs are miserable little brutes and I knew one hog would not last three lion long. So there seemed nothing for it but to close in quickly and try to bag at least two of the brutes.

There were only small isolated bushes here beside the kraal because this place had been cleared a year or two before and probably planted. There was a small bush in front of me and about seven strides from the lion, and just beyond the lion stood two or three small thorn bushes whose branches had interlocked some three feet from the ground, forming a small tunnel. Beyond this the open ground extended to the edge of the scrub, about fifteen yards away. To my right, the ground was bare until it met the scrub and a big baobab tree, about fifteen or twenty yards away. The village lay behind my left shoulder and the open ground extended for another twenty-five yards or so to my half-left front. The villagers, about 150 of them, men, women and children, were clustered in a half-circle from not quite broad on my left, around behind me, and over to nearly broad on my right. The fellow with the shotgun was over on my left.

It might seem madness to open fire on a bunch of three maneaters with such a concourse of natives close around like that, and it certainly would have been asking for trouble if they had been ordinary hunting lion. They were, however, the definitely would-be maneaters, one of which had tried to kill a woman shortly before. The study of maneaters, be they lion, tiger or leopard, is fascinating, if only because these abnormal animals so completely alter their habits and general outlook. It is now well known that if you open fire on a troop —or "pride", as they like to call it—of ordinary hunting lion, and there are females amongst them, you can expect to be charged. You may not be, but you must allow for it because it is quite usual. In the case of maneaters, the position is quite different. These abnormal beasts seem to know quite well that they are doing wrong. The hunting lion knows that he hasn't interfered with man, and therefore if man opens fire on him he may resent it—or, rather, one of the females may; but in the case of maneaters it would seem that they are fully aware that this time it is they who have started the ball rolling and that man, the relatives of the victim, is quite entitled to seek vengeance. I cannot recollect a single maneater or his mate that charged me before being wounded. Furthermore, it must be remembered that the lion in Africa are not accustomed to being shot at, and missed or wounded, as are tiger in India. Apart from myself, it is rare for anybody to hunt these maneaters in Africa nowadays.

I felt pretty certain that the discharge of a powerful rifle at such close quarters would have a most disconcerting effect; in addition to the fact that my being so close would make it look as though I had no fear of them at all, as indeed I had not. I used to feel afraid, but subsequent experience showed me that I must put fear behind me if I was to be successful in my hunting. My job was to scare the lions.

Crouching slightly so as to keep that little bush between me and the lion, I walked quickly and quietly up to it. All three lion, the usual combination of a male and two females, were lying down and were so concentrated on stuffing themselves with stolen hog that not one of them noticed me. Since I was scarcely seven strides away from the nearest of them and, standing up, was in a position to shoot down on them, I felt a head shot was permissible. The lion was facing directly away from me; one lioness was over on my left; and the other facing me.

I placed my bullet on the base of the lion's skull just where the neck bone joins it. It killed him instantly. At the shot the lioness on my left sprang back and a piece of the bush beside which I was standing prevented my getting a clear shot at her. The other lioness whipped around and dashed back through that little tunnel I mentioned. When she reached the open ground she halted again and looked back. I dropped to one knee so as to shoot through the tunnel. It was a somewhat tricky shot because of the angle at which the lioness was standing, but I took it because I expected to hear the old shotgun of the half-caste fire.

I slipped my bullet close past the lioness's jaw and so into her chest, just inside and slightly above the point of her shoulder. I hoped that it would rake through the big main arteries at the top of her heart. The impact of the heavy bullet brought her down; but in an instant she had scrambled to her feet and dashed blindly away across the open to my right. I felt fairly certain of her. As I reloaded, sure enough, came the report of a shotgun over on my left, and an easily-identifiable yell from the half-caste: "I've hit her, I've hit her!" The second lioness bounded clear over the hog and dead lion and thus got across the open ground to my right. When closing that little bush just before opening fire, I had as usual slipped between my lips the whistle which always hangs on a thong around my neck. I now blew a shrill blast on the whistle.

Whether it was this sound, or whether the lioness would have pulled up anyway on the edge of the scrub for a last look back, I naturally cannot say. An unwounded lion will very often look round, but this lioness had been peppered with buckshot. Anyway, she pulled up as I hoped she would, just as I was closing the breech after reloading. I feel sure I could have killed that lioness there and then if I'd been alone; but the half-caste loosed off his old gun again, and yelled: "I've hit her again. I've hit her again!" The lioness whipped around and leapt into the grass and scrub before I could get my sights on her.

I handed my rifle to the nearest native—lest I should do murder with it—and in three explosive leaps reached the gunman. I bestowed upon him the one good kick that relieved outraged temper, my only regret being that I was only shod with rubber-soled canvas shoes. Not only had he driven the lioness away and lost me an almost certain shot at her; but that second charge of buckshot had whistled unpleasantly close past my shoulder and head.

"So you've hit her—have you? And hit her again?" I shouted. "Well, then, get after her with your damned shotgun! Do you think I'm going to follow-up in that scrub a lioness *you've* twice wounded? Follow her up yourself!"

The half-caste had, of course, no intention of doing so. I had to consider my next step. I did not believe the lioness was seriously hurt. The half-caste had shot at her from both sides, but the lioness was still travelling on all fours when I last saw her. There was only one tiny speck of blood where she had stood at the edge of the grass before disappearing.

Feeling certain I'd find the first lioness dead, I'd a hunch that the second one might halt for a moment beside her; then, when she realised she was dead, she would move on. But, knowing these brutes as I did, I thought there was more than a fair chance that she would return to look for the lion that night shortly after dark. She would be more interested in him and his whereabouts and fate than she would in the other lioness. Consequently, if I failed to find her close to where I expected to find the first lioness, it would be better not to attempt to follow her up. The scrub and the nature of the ground did not lend themselves to spooring a soft-footed animal; and if I let her see that I was too interested in her she might clear off entirely and be very difficult to pick up again. It would be a much wiser policy to wait for nightfall and try for her then.

No animal could possibly have lived long after shedding the quantity of blood the first lioness had—in great dollops and splashes along her spoor. It was clear that the bullet had done all I had hoped it would do. Still, I am a firm believer in the old bushman's axiom that none of these critters can be reckoned dead until you have its hide pegged out. What was really so remarkable was that the first lioness had been able to get to her feet and dash away after being knocked down and so wounded. It shows the vitality and tenacity-to-life of members of the cat family, and the stupidity of those who go hunting them in thick cover with small-bore rifles.

I found the first lioness about twenty-five yards within the scrub; and then moved around very quietly to see if I could spot the second lioness. Her spoor showed that she had passed close to her dead comrade, stopped for a hasty glance at her, and then slipped away into the surrounding scrub. There was no blood on the spoor, so I did not pursue her then.

After the first lioness and the lion had been skinned, I had the two carcasses dumped down together. The second lioness was nearly sure to come looking for her mate, and since there had not been time to eat a great deal of the hog before I opened fire, I knew the lioness must still be hungry. Lion don't hesitate to eat a dead companion if they can find nothing else, and indeed will sometimes do so even if there is other meat there as well.

I didn't intend to sit up for the second lioness as there was no suitable tree in the vicinity. I could, of course, have had the bait brought closer to the baobab tree, but, it would have meant sitting up very high, and I much prefer to get my shot from ground-level if I can. It is very much easier to get a bullet into a vital spot if you are on the same level as your prey rather than shoot from far above him.

The day passed as such days do. When the light had gone I clamped my flashlight to the left barrel of my rifle and made my way up the hill. All was silent in the village. I had warned the villagers not to hang about after dark, but to get into their huts and stay there. I walked slowly past the big baobab tree, swinging the beam of my flashlight around in a wide arc—not forgetting the occasional sweep behind me. But no glowing eyes were to be seen. The red eyes of doves; and the ruby eyes of nightjars; and here and there the scintillating bright eyes of a spider, like two flawless little diamonds. That was all. Clearly I had come too soon: I returned to camp, but rather less than an hour later I again climbed the hill. This time my hopes were raised for a moment when I saw an animal feeding on the bait. But it was only a hyena; the green flash I noticed when he moved his head told me so even before I was close enough to see him clearly. There is no green flash or glint in a lion's eyes as there frequently is in those of a tiger or leopard. From the fact that the hyena was feeding on the bait I knew that the lioness couldn't be in the immediate vicinity. So once more I dropped down the hill to my camp.

Eleven times during the night I made my pilgrimage up the hill without catching so much as a glimpse of that much-wanted lioness. And then as I prepared for the twelfth and last time, I calculated that day would be breaking by the time I arrived at the bait and that the flashlight would therefore be a mere encumbrance, so I left it behind. But I'd miscalculated slightly, because when I reached the baobab I found that I could not see my gun sights sufficiently clearly. Accordingly, since this was a maneater I was hunting—at least, practically a maneater—I got the comforting fat trunk of the tree behind me. There was a slight recess into which I wedged myself, and the bole of the tree was about ten feet in diameter. This gave me a pleasant feeling of security. Anything that wanted to get at me would have to approach from more or less directly in front of me. But nothing moved. I remained quite motionless there until I could see my sights well enough to shoot, and then very slowly and quietly stalked the bait.

And this time the gods had relented. There was my lioness— it could only be the third maneater—standing nearly broadside-on to me and gazing down contemplatively at the carcases of her two erstwhile mates, one of which had been badly mangled by hyenas. I am quite sure the lioness could not have heard the shot that killed her. She dropped in her tracks. There was no need for the second bullet that, to be on the safe side, I sent crashing in through the top of her head as she lay on her side with her back towards me.

The Lifumba Buffalo

BELOW the Lupata Gorge, through which the Zambezi hurls itself, the country opens out and flattens. Six or eight miles beyond the lower entrance to the gorge and on the North bank of the river, you come to the lagoon of Lifumba. It is an L-shaped lake with the longer arm of the L running more or less at right angles to the river. The lagoon is connected to the river by a narrow channel overgrown with *Matetti*, a tall tough cane-like growth, and long coarse grass; but since hippo often make use of this channel, they have deepened it so that it is possible to take a canoe or even a small boat through it.

In the angle formed by the two arms of the lake there is a patch of forest with a lot of dense undergrowth but with reasonably clear patches here and there amid the denseness. The ground is sandy loam and stoneless. Rhino live in there, and a considerable number of old buffalo bulls which have been wounded in the past and consequently lost their leadership in the various herds which frequent this district at certain periods of the year. These animals all spend the daylight hours in this forest, only coming out after sundown to feed around the edge of the lake and enjoy their mud-baths. At daybreak they return to their sanctuary. For sanctuary that forest had always been for them in the past. The local natives told me that none of the pseudo-hunters who had previously tried to work this district would venture into that forest more than perhaps twenty or twenty-five yards, but I had a job to do and meant to penetrate as far as necessary.

Apart from these old bulls, which live here all through the year, the herds normally live in the many valleys throughout the range of hills through which the Zambezi has cut its way. Up there the buffalo live in family parties and small herds. When, however, the grass dries up and also the water and mudbaths, which buffalo simply must have, they are compelled to come down to the flat country around Lifumba, since that is the only place left where they can find enough to live on. Here they combine into immense herds numbering many hundreds of animals. If they confined themselves to what nature has provided for them, well and good; but unfortunately they persist in raiding the local natives' food crops and cotton gardens. No one who has not actually seen it can have any conception of the devastation the herds can cause over-night: they literally sweep the ground bare—they don't even leave the stalks. Again and again I have seen fine standing crops of maize and cotton as I passed during the evening shortly before sundown; and then, when I returned the following morning in response to a frantic S O S , there would be nothing but the bare ground covered with buffalo spoor, tracks and dung. An entire year's food supply for several families wiped out overnight.

I spent four months a year for five consecutive years here shooting back these marauders, punishing them for their trespass, and thinning out the herds. The meat of the slain would be some compensation to the natives for the loss of their crops: they would eat a lot, but they would dry most of it and carry it away to barter for grain in some other district that had not suffered from similar depredations.

These buffalo are classed as vermin because of the inestimable damage they do and because they are by far the worst carriers and spreaders of the dreaded tsetse fly. Both varieties are death to all domestic animals, and one variety brings death, in the form of sleeping sickness (trypanosomiasis), to human beings. Admittedly, when the rains commence and the herds break up into their smaller groups and return to their respective valleys whence they came, they take most of the fly with them; but inevitably and invariably they leave fly where no fly was to be found before, and increase the fly in those parts that were previously infested.

I found this buffalo-hunting intensely interesting and gained great experience and knowledge of their habits, and learned how to go about hunting them. Of course, it will be understood that I was hunting professionally and was therefore out for quantity rather than quality.

During the early part of the season it was necessary to hunt them by day since the district was covered with long grass varying from five to seven feet high. However, after the big herds had been wandering around for a while they trampled it down to a great extent, and one could then make a big killing sometimes by night with the aid of a good shooting lamp. I did not often wander far looking for them by night; but whenever they came around my camp or around one of my temporary bivouacs I would shoot when I could. I believe I was the first if not the only hunter who ever attempted to tackle them in that manner. As night shooting takes place at ranges varying between fifteen and twenty-five yards, there is no excuse for not killing clean with every shot. If it is one of the smaller parties containing from thirty to perhaps sixty head, there is nothing to worry about; but when tackling one of the really big herds it is necessary to keep an eye roving around on both sides of you because those animals in the rear ranks will be barging their way up close to see what it is all about, and will inevitably spread around on both sides of you. This could easily mean that sooner or later some of them may get your wind and stampede. When the others hear that, even though dazzled by your lamp, they will probably also make a rush. Then it is a certainty that at some stage of the proceedings one or more will put their noses down to sniff at the carcase of one of their mates which you have shot and which is lying at their feet, but which, through being blinded by the lamp, they have not yet realised is dead. The instant they get the smell of the freshly-spilt blood they will take off like scalded cats. And, like all game, if one goes the others go too. If it is one of the smaller parties there is little or no danger provided you don't let yourself get all steamed-up. In the case of one of the really big herds having spread around you, however, you may find yourself and your gunbearer more or less in the middle of a frantic mass stampede. Since you cannot be looking or have your shooting lamp in more than one direction at the same time, many of those buff won't be dazzled and so can see you. They can also see the other animals clearing off. I found it a good thing to give my gunbearer a flashlight to carry and use in these circumstances. It was then possible to keep the vast majority of the buff dazzled all the time.

I remember shooting-up a fairly big herd one night when they came around my bivouac. I had been called to a native kraal some three miles from my base camp where the crops had been severely damaged. I followed the raiders and punished them during the midday hours. This is usually by far the best time. If you get after them too early you will catch up with them while they are still moving, and all you will see are their hindquarters. This applies to elephant and rhino as well as to buffalo. But when the sun warms up they mostly seek out some place in which to lie up in whatever shade they can find; though in the case of a really big herd they can seldom find sufficient shade and will often be found in the centre of some big open burnt-off plain.

The grass had not yet been fired here, however, and I found

c

them on the edge of the scrub. As in all good buffalo country, the soil here was very rich and carried much long grass and "buffalo bean" interspersed with clumps of bush and palmetto. Most, though not all, of the trees were palms. There is nothing much more to say about the punishing of that herd: it was all perfectly straightforward. When I was satisfied that I had taught them a lesson I returned to the kraal and chatted with the headman who glorified in the name of "Frying Pan". I had known him for years.

He told me that there were at least two, and possibly three, different herds that came raiding fairly regularly here. I was quite prepared to believe that, because I had seen buffalo spoor on all sides when nearing the kraal and when I went out to pick up the tracks of the raiders. Accordingly, I promised to camp by a small clearing about half a mile from the kraal. I had passed it earlier and noticed that herds of buffalo seemed to cross backwards and forwards there pretty often. There was water in it and a small circular patch of light bush near the centre with a clear place in the middle of it. It would be very suitable for a bivouac.

At this season there would be no rain, so I didn't bother about tents. My men and I took it easy during the afternoon and evening. Since the spoor I had examined in the clearing had shown that buffalo had crossed and recrossed here nightly during the past several nights, I felt reasonably sure that they would come by again that night. And since the professional hunter gets all the walking any man in his right mind could possibly want—and a good deal more than that!—in the ordinary course of his work, I would be more than glad of the opportunity of shooting up this herd without any walking at all.

So, after having my evening meal, I told my fellows to let the fire die out as soon as they had finished cooking theirs.

Thereafter they lay down and soon were deep in the Land of Nod. My gunbearer and I sat on, sipping our strong black coffee and smoking, I my pipe and he his homemade cheroots. We chatted quietly of this and that, and viewed Life and the World as seen through African eyes. There was no chance of the buffalo arriving unbeknown to us, hearing us, and decamping without our knowledge. In this district the herds made a tremendous noise at night when wandering around and feeding: they grunted and snorted and rattled their horns together. The clashing and rattling of the horns of a large herd could be heard for a considerable distance. There can be no doubt that all this was in the hope of discouraging lion from attacking them. You did not hear any such noises by day, and lion very, very seldom attack buffalo in daylight.

It was, I suppose, somewhere between eight and nine when we first heard them. They were definitely approaching. I fixed the five-cell shooting lamp on my forehead, switched it on, and adjusted it so that it would show up my sights when aiming. I then switched it out and waited. I would have liked to use a pair of short-barrelled magazine rifles with my gunbearer reloading for me; but unfortunately here in Portuguese East Africa we are restricted to three rifles only (two if we don't hunt elephant), and since most of my shooting is done with double rifles, I have two of them and only the one light magazine, a Mauser. Accordingly, I decided to use my pair of doubles with Saduko reloading for me. This is an excellent practice when conditions permit; but not quite so good at night because with one's eyes on the game one cannot see the second rifle out of the corner of one's eye when exchanging as one can by day. However, my man had been with me for years, ever since he was a youngster, and I had trained him myself. He was absolutely staunch and reliable, never let me down, and always had my second rifle ready and held out in the best possible position for me to grab should I want it in a hurry.

The herd was being very accommodating. Buffalo almost invariably work upwind at night, presumably so as not to blunder into danger; and it might almost be described as a definite characteristic of theirs to stampede downwind. On this occasion had the herd been coming directly upwind they would almost certainly have winded us, because we were more than a third of the way out in the little clear patch. To my delight, however, they were cutting slightly across the wind and so had no notion of our existance. I waited until nearly half the herd had passed and then walked towards them with my shooting lamp switched on. I needn't really have walked towards them at all, as they were only about twenty-five or at most thirty yards away. However, I took ten or a dozen strides towards them and halted. Naturally, the entire herd also stopped and gazed towards the light. They had never seen such a thing before and were wondering what it was.

My first shot I slammed through the shoulder of a very big bull, dropping him instantly. They were still nearly all broadside-on to me. At the shot they now swung around and stood looking directly towards me. So my next shot was a frontal brain-shot; and I knew that most if not all subsequent shots would be similar. The second beast dropped in his tracks, and I exchanged rifles. It was now a case of picking a target and firing just as quickly as I could, swinging on to another, firing, and exchanging rifles with my gunbearer. Both weapons were fitted with ejectors which slung out the fired shells, so that my bearer was usually able to have my second weapon ready when I wanted it. This worked well, although, as I have already mentioned, I rather think a pair of short Mausers might have been better.

After the third shot the entire herd commenced edging towards me, jostling one another and crowding together. They didn't hurry: they just took a pace or two and then halted again. But the jostling continued all the time. As they came closer, naturally they had to avoid those I had slain. It is strange how sometimes it takes a long time for any of them to smell the blood. As far as the first one was concerned, the one I had shot through the shoulder, there probably wasn't any blood for them to smell. He had, as is usually the case, fallen on the side on which he had received the bullet, doubtless because that shoulder had given way first. The others were all frontal brain-shots and there is normally a thick gout of dark blood from the mouth with such shots. Eventually I had the herd within ten yards of me, and still I continued to shoot. But now I took three or four paces backwards and away from them as Saduko whispered that a number of the buffalo were working up on my right. If I allowed them to come around too far they would get our wind. So, having taken up a new position, I swung around to face those and opened fire on them; and then swung around again and dropped another two from those in the centre. As I did so, there came a sudden snort from some beast immediately beyond them. I saw a huge black bulk that took a mighty leap over something, doubtless the body of one of the fallen. With his tail curled up over his back, he dashed away. Obviously he had at last had a whiff of fresh blood. With that, the remainder of the herd also wheeled around and took off. I got in two quick shots as they exposed their broadsides, and then they were gone.

Naturally, my men were all awake after the first shot. They had had a fine grandstand view of the battle and they went around collecting tails, shouting joyfully to one another as they found the carcases. Of course, they did not have far to look because the shooting had all been at such close range and

I knew that there were no wounded. Altogether they brought in twenty-two tails. And, since I had bagged nine that morning, whether or not it was the same herd, Frying Pan and his people would do well. I and my men took as many tongues as we wanted to keep us going in fresh meat, and, had we wanted it, would have taken the fat from one of the beasts. But we had enough to go on with and could get plenty more as required.

Of course, there is no "sport" in this kind of shooting; but I was here to help my African friends, not in search of sport alone. I wanted to help not only the locals, but also those who would come in their scores from over the Nyasaland border to buy meat. These men, having sold their cash crops (either cotton or tobacco or both) would come down with their own porters and buy buffalo from me. They would pay cash over the carcase and then have their men cut up the beast, smoke the big strips of fine meat, and tote it all back to their homes to retail there. I fixed the prices so that they could double their money. This helped them and pleased them greatly. Although at the beginning of the season they might only have enough money to buy one or two buffalo, by the end of the season they would be buying ten, twelve or fifteen apiece on each trip. This was, of course, entirely legitimate because after the crops had been harvested—that is, such crops as were left —there was no more raiding because there was nothing for the buffaloes to raid. Nevertheless, their numbers had to be kept down. There were far too many of them and they were breeding like the proverbial rabbits. Practically every cow, other than the very old ones, had a calf at heel, while many of the cows would also be in calf unless the youngster with her was very young.

I remember a rather curious sight one morning when following up a herd of raiders. I had bivouaced in a small outlying kraal near the hills which had been suffering badly from marauders. I had not been able to get here before as there had been so many calls from the centre of the district. However, at last I was able to manage it before the natives were eaten completely out of house and home.

Most of the villagers slept on raised platforms in their lands and would beat drums and rattle stones in tin cans in an attempt to drive off any marauders. When therefore, early in the night I heard the drums and shouts of the men, women and children, I awakened my gunbearer and together we made our way out there. The buffalo were so accustomed to all the racket made by the musicians that they did not take much notice of it: they merely refrained from approaching too close to the noise, but they continued feeding elsewhere through the maize or millet as the case might be.

I wanted to shoot a large number of the marauders so as to impress upon the survivors that it was inadvisable to raid, and to make my attack, it was necessary to get right around to the far side of the lands and enter them on the tracks of the raiders. This would not only put me downwind of them, but would also give me a clear field of fire. Otherwise, the twelve to fifteen-foot millet stalks, planted as they are in clusters, would seriously interfere. I got close up to them and opened fire. I had no difficulty in slaying a dozen or so, but then the survivors decided to break away. Since it was a fairly big herd and came raiding here regularly, I determined to follow them up next morning.

According to my invariable custom, I had a good breakfast which I knew would keep me going until sundown when I would have my second and only other meal of the day. Throughout the day I might take fruit if there was any, but otherwise I did not eat, though I would drink tea or coffee. Not only is a heavy midday meal a mistake in very hot districts, since it makes one drowsy and disinclined for work, but it is precisely during those hottest hours of the day that one ought to be hunting the big fellows. I had long learned my lesson.

The spoor of the raiders led us right up along the edge of the foothills for several miles—they must have got a considerable scare there in the lands when I shot them up. However, they probably got over their fright eventually when they found they were not being followed. They began to swing round, climbed up quite a bit, and then commenced to retrace their steps along the side of the rise more or less parallel with their outward route. We came to a place where something had startled them, possibly a wandering lion or pair of lion which they winded. As here they suddenly broke into a gallop, as their spoor clearly showed. They had stampeded along the side of the hill, which was pretty open, only having light scattered trees amongst scattered rocks and boulders. The grass was thin and short here so that visibility was good. I was astonished to see a young buffalo, either a heifer or a young bull, standing all by itself right in the centre of the broad track left by the stampeding herd. It was quite motionless except for the occasional swishing of its tail, and it made no move even when we were quite close. This was unusual, but I saw what had happened. The buffalo was wedged between two trees which seemed to be growing up from the same root system. They had formed a V and the young buff's neck was fairly jammed in the V, as securely held as some cow in a milking byre. Its horns prevented it drawing back, and its shoulders and body could not push through. It was apparent that the young buffalo must have been squeezed off the ground by the press of mature animals on both sides and been carried along until they reached this tree or pair of trees. The herd had passed on either side of the obstacle, thereby allowing the younger animal to drop to the ground, but unfortunately for it the others did not drop it soon enough, and so the buffalo was jammed. The result was what we found. The heifer, as I found it to be, was unhurt and unmarked. It was a good thing for her that we had arrived on the scene before some of the carnivora. The wretched animal would have been unable to do anything to help herself or protect herself and she might well have been eaten alive by hyenas that coming night or the following one. It is extremely doubtful if even a lion could have killed the buffalo in the position in which she was held.

I killed her myself, both because it was my job to kill as many of these buff as I could and because she would be fat as butter and beautifully tender.

I then continued after the herd and completed the lesson I had commenced to teach them the previous night.

Men get queer ideas about buffalo. Most men without much experience seem to think that buff will attack without any provocation. Others believe that a buff will invariably whip around on feeling the lead and make a savage and determined charge. Well, all I can say to that is that I have never experienced either of these things, and I have shot and killed close to twelve hundred buffalo, and, of course, to have shot so many, I have encountered possibly a hundred times that number.

Of course, a wounded buffalo is something very different. When you follow him into long grass or thick bush he may indeed charge you, but then you will be expecting that. The answer is: DON'T WOUND. Take care to place your bullet, your *first* bullet, in the right spot and you have nothing to worry about. All too many men are inclined to get excited when they see their quarry there in front of them and cannot resist the temptation to open fire immediately. But the whole art of hunting is to use your bushcraft so as to defeat the animal on his own ground. If this is properly carried out there should be little or no difficulty in the actual shot: it is just the finishing touch, the final consummation. It ought to make no difference whether you are an amateur hunting for a good trophy, or whether you are a professional whose livelihood it is. Admittedly, in the case of the latter it may all too often mean shooting for quantity; but my experience has been throughout the thirty-five years I was hunting professionally that it pays over and over again to place one's *first* shot accurately in the right place. It saves innumerable unpleasant and dangerous follow-ups, when one might be hunting other beasts; and it saves endless time and energy to be accurate.

The Nsungu Maneaters

Just above the upper entrance to the Lupata Gorge on the Zambezi there is a place called Nsungu on the North bank. A little conical hill lies quite close to the river on which I always camped when passing either upstream or down. There are no trees or bush on the little hill; but on it are two small huts, one intended for a bedroom and the other for a kitchen, and also a *mecheza*. This was a conical thatched roof on stilts, without any walls and intended to be used as dining and sitting room. This little camp was built by the local villagers for the Chefe de Poste (local administrative officer) for use on his rare visits. I used the huts whenever I was there.

I always liked that camp. To the east stood the sheer vertical cliffs forming the mouth of the gorge. In the centre stood a large island identical with the cliffs on both sides and very nearly as high. These sheer cliffs blaze red-bronze in the light of the setting sun. Then, opposite them, you are privileged to gaze in awe and humility at the indescribable beauty of a perfect Zambezi sunset. As the great red ball of the sun sinks into the upper reaches of the broad river and the marvellous after-glow slowly fades, you may see a large grey heron slowly winging his way homeward. Comes the deep sonorous laugh of an old bull hippo followed by the high-pitched snort of one of his cows, and presently the sing-song roar of a lion perhaps half a mile away.

It was these lion that had brought me here this time. Word had reached me that they had created a positive reign of terror from Nsungu here to Kasanya, further up the river; and also between Nsungu and Chimbidzi and beyond. Chimbidzi lies up along the valley which runs down at right angles from the north. Nsungu is situated, as it were, at the mouth of this valley which, however, has opened out considerably a mile or more before reaching the river.

But although the maneating lion were by far the worst, there were also some very bad crocs here. The entire Zambezi is well known for its maneating crocs. They are to be found throughout its vast length, but Nsungu and Bandari, the upper and lower entrances respectively to the Gorge, are notorious. As my canoe drew in to the landing place that midday I was about to put a foot over the side with the intention of washing it (I always travel barefoot when afloat), but the natives on the bank shouted to me not to do so because two women had been taken there by crocs only an hour or so before.

Shortly afterwards, when I was enjoying a pot of tea on my little hill, we heard two or three yells from the river bank at the foot of the hill. I grabbed a rifle as a matter of course, though I knew only too well that I would be much too late, and dashed down the hill with my men. When we got there all we found was some wretched man's loin-cloth and his little tomahawk. Evidently he had stripped with the intention of taking a bath and was probably standing in water just over his ankles or maybe halfway up his shins when he was grabbed. That spelt three victims within as many hours. Surely the unfortunate man must have been a stranger passing through: I can scarcely believe that any of the locals would have been quite so stupid as to take a bath in such a dangerous spot.

I shot a very big croc close by that evening. There was a small sandbank not very far offshore and I saw the brute pull himself up on to it. He was facing directly away from me, and since I was considerably above him, offered a perfect shot. It was a very long shot at a croc, in spite of his size. The vital areas are not large, but I was using a very accurate rifle fitted with a peep sight. I placed my bullet in the base of his skull and killed him instantly. He gave a convulsive jump, his tail coming right over his back and almost meeting his upthrown snout, and then lay quivering, his tail trying to drive him still further up on the sandbank.

When he was cut open many native ornaments, beads, brass bangles and anklets etc. were found in his belly, so there was no possible doubt of his maneating proclivities. Of course, there was no means of knowing if he had been responsible for any of the three killings that day. It is generally believed that crocs store their victims in some underwater hidyhole and leave them there until decomposition has commenced. I am inclined to accept this theory as being highly probable. A croc's teeth are clearly designed for biting and holding: they are round and pointed and widely separated, and there are no molars for chewing. Moreover, he has no tongue—not a vestige.

A shark's teeth, on the contrary, are equally obviously designed for biting and slicing or shearing. A shark has an enormous gullet which enables him to swallow anything, such as a limb, that he has bitten off; but a croc's gullet is comparatively small. When decomposition has started it would be easy for the croc to pull the body to pieces. Accordingly, this brute may well have been guilty of killing at least one, if not more, of those who lost their lives this day. The fact that no fresh meat was found in his stomach means nothing, as we have seen.

Although I naturally shoot these maneating crocs whenever I get the chance, it was the maneating lion I wanted. I gathered from the local headman who came to visit me, and who had been responsible for the SOS which had brought me here, that there were usually three of the brutes in the vicinity, but that sometimes five had been seen. He could not say whether or not it was the one party that occasionally broke up into two lots or whether there were really three lots of them in the district, one being a trio and another a pair, and then a third lot of five. Anyway, for the past nine months they had been plagued by these brutes. At first the killings had only taken place at the usual times: sundown, daybreak, or during the night. The victims had by no means all been locals. There was a fairly considerable number of natives from up-river and from down who passed through here on their way to the Township of Tete and when returning therefrom. This being a very hot district many of these travellers used to pass through on moonlight nights so as to avoid walking through the heat of the day. They were a gift for the maneaters. Naturally, word quickly flew up and down along the route, and thereafter night traffic ceased. The walkers made a point of getting through the danger area in daylight.

But still the killings continued. Africans just don't seem to be able to realise that maneating lion seldom attempt a second killing in the same place immediately. After securing a victim they usually wander from twelve to twenty miles before trying for another. They seem to know that the survivors of the attack will redouble their precautions so that it will be extremely difficult for them to bag another just then. The African being what he is, however, when there have been two or three or four successive nights without any alarm he begins to relax those precautions and again take chances. Accordingly, when the lion return they have little or no difficulty in securing a feed. This will continue for weeks and even months. To the African there is no such thing as natural death: it must be witchcraft. Maneaters, whether lion, leopard or croc, are always some witch or wizard who has transformed himself into a maneater so as to get his own back on someone who has done him a bad turn. A native decides he hasn't done anyone a bad turn, so why should he worry? no harm will come to him. Eventually, of course, as the killings continue, the natives then realise that this is something unusual: they shut themselves into their huts long before the sun is down and take care to remain within until long after the sun is well up.

That is what happened here. And then came the most extraordinary and unusual happenings: the lion, finding themselves unable to secure human kills by night, took to killing by day. They would sneak up on some unsuspecting woman working in her lands and carry her off. It happened again and again until the distracted villagers had to work each other's lands on a communal basis: that is, the entire village would work someone's garden today, and then on each successive day they would all work in someone else's, and so on. They had to go in strong parties to fetch dry sticks for the cooking fires and for water, the men armed with their useless little spears and their tomahawks.

The lion, and I saw their spoor myself later, would now take possession of some kraal throughout the night and just wander around and lie there in the clear and open places between the huts and in the centre of the kraal. Some of them would actually lie on the little step outside the door of some hut and wait for one of the occupants to come out. They would even go so far as to shove a paw through the wall of the hut, if they could, or around the edge of the reed door, for all the world as though they were trying to awaken one of the occupants in the hope that he or she would come out. Yet, strangely enough, they didn't attempt to break in through the grass-thatched roof. I don't know why—I have known other maneaters do so. I also don't know why these brutes should have taken to maneating in the first place. There was plenty of game around Nsungu, mostly waterbuck, but there were also reedbuck and any number of warthog—one of the lion's favourite foods. Chimbidzi by its very name—the place of Zebra—indicates that the lion's other favourite was plentiful there. Besides, I had several times hunted around Chimbidzi and knew in addition to zebra there were also plenty of lesser kudu and sable antelope not far away as well as the ubiquitous warthog. Admittedly, there wasn't so much game between Nsungu and Kasanya—just a few waterbuck and lesser kudu; but then there was nothing to take the lion up there if they hadn't wanted to go. They could have lived quite happily between Nsungu and Chimbidzi and beyond. There was always plenty of game right up through that country: away up through Tangaranutchi, where you—or the lion—could bear north into Tuia's country which swarms with game. Yet they didn't: they deliberately came down here and commenced maneating. There is no explanation.

I had arrived by canoe. I had no motor transport in those days. In any case there was no road that anything bigger than a jeep could have driven along, and jeeps were not yet known. My difficulty now was to contact these brutes. There was a vast amount of thick bush lying between Nsungu and Kasanya much of it thorn, and not many people living there. There were quite a few kraals around Nsungu and then none until one approached Chimbidzi. There were several scattered around there, and then another gap. But curiously enough the maneaters did not go beyond the last of the kraals in the Chimbidzi area, although there was a longer uninhabited stretch between Chimbidzi and Nsungu than there was between Chimbidzi and the nearest of the next group of kraals.

For the present at any rate, I intended to remain here in Nsungu as it was definitely the most central. The headman sent out word in all directions to tell folks that I was there and had come to help; and that they were to send runners to let me know of all kills or if the lion had been seen.

It was an awkward and very difficult district in which to hunt lion, especially maneaters, because the ground was hard-baked by the sun (it was the latter part of the dry season). Around Chimbidzi the country consisted of steeply-undulating ground covered with loose round stones over which it would be impossible to spoor a soft-footed animal and over which it was extremely difficult to walk quietly. In some places they had already commenced firing the grass, and my first instructions were that the grass was to be burned off everywhere. That would not only give me a better view when hunting, but it would greatly simplify spooring except over those infernal stones. However, even there it would help because there were occasional small patches where the stones were not quite so close together and where it would then be possible to see tracks, if my quarry happened to pass that way. Then again, the inhabited district was L-shaped. There was nobody living in the bush that filled the angle formed by the two arms of the L because there was no water there. Wherever there is permanent water in Africa you will find natives and the natural corollary to that is that where there are no natives there is no water, other perhaps than in the rains.

While pondering over these matters I began to see how I should set about hunting down the maneaters. Although the lion might sometimes lie up in that large area of bush, I did not think it likely that they would spend much time in there. It being quite evident that they preferred Man to their natural quarry they would be much more likely to spend their off-time in or near those parts in which they could find humans. Furthermore, I knew that all lion, be they maneaters or otherwise, preferred walking along roads and paths when getting from one place to another rather than cutting through the

D

bush. The paths had all been beaten out by the bare feet of countless natives throughout the centuries and therefore there was far less likelihood of either men or lion picking up thorns in their feet when walking along them. So with that in mind I rather doubted if these maneaters would cut through the bush when getting from one end of their beat to the other. They would find nothing to interest them in the bush, which was full of thorns. If I was right it would greatly reduce my difficulties.

Another very considerable asset in my favour was that these lion had almost certainly never heard a rifle speak, much less had they ever been shot at or wounded. Against that, however, was the fact that they would not return to a kill, assuming they had left any of it. A single human being, and most of the kills were single, would not in any case be much for five lion.

Another order I had the headman pass along was that no drums were to be beaten, either by day or by night, except the recognised signal telling of an attack by lion. If you have ever heard that series of rolls and taps you can never mistake it: it is extraordinarily like a lion's sing-song roar in the distance.

As the sun was dropping, the headman left to go down the hill to his home. It was still far too dangerous for him to be out and about so late. My sympathies went out to these un-fortunate people who for months past had had to shut them-selves into their huts while it was still broad day instead of sitting around talking and gossiping and discussing the day's happenings, as Africans love to do. After all, they have no other entertainment in the evenings: no cinemas, no radios, no theatres, no concerts, no television. When the moon is full they will dance and sing, perhaps, throughout the greater part of the night; if not, they will just prolong their chats with the children, laughing and playing, making up for the lethargy of the hot midday hours. Whereas now, long before the sun reached the horizon, one might think the entire district was dead, wiped out by some deadly plague. Not a soul to be seen moving about anywhere, not a sound indicating the existence of a human being, just a wisp of blue smoke climbing through the thatch of the roofs as the evening meal was being prepared.

I only had three men with me: my gunbearer, cook, and a youngster to help him. The cook and the lad would sleep in the kitchen; my gunbearer always shared my sleeping quarters so that I could instantly awaken him should I need him during the night. Up here on the little hill we had a good view all around. There was therefore little likelihood of our being taken unawares by the maneaters should they take it into their heads to drift up our way. So we did not shut ourselves up when the locals did. However, since there was a certain amount of light bush growing around the north and east sides of the little hill, and reaching to within some ten or twelve yards of the top, which formed ample cover for a lion if one did not happen to be watching carefully all the time, I decided it would be inadvisable for my fellows to sit around after dark. I would have that bush cleared back next day.

Somewhere in the middle of the night I awoke, quite certain I had heard a drum. I lay still for a moment, listening, because the drummers pause for a short while between each series of calls. Sure enough, it came again and from the kraal at the foot of our hill. I woke Saduko and slipped on a pair of shoes. Then I strapped my shooting lamp on and, taking my rifle, made my way down to where the drum was still being beaten. I had swung the beam of the lamp around when emerging from the hut—just in case; but I switched it out again when descending the hill, as I did not want to let the lion know that I was coming. When I reached the foot of the hill I switched it on again. The kraal was only some twenty-five or thirty yards from the foot of the hill. I made straight

for it. It was a scattered collection of huts without any fence
around it, but roughly in the centre there was the usual open
space with the customary palaver-house in the middle. The
palaver-house is merely a larger edition of a *macheza*: it's
quite open. As I later learned, one of the lion had approached
the reed door of one of the huts and must have pushed its
nose close to it and sniffed. It had also loosed a deep sigh. That
had been enough for the occupants. One of them had called
out, warning everyone that the lion had arrived and telling
the drummer to send out the signal so that I would hear. The
drummer, of course, had his drum in the hut with him.

As I approached the open space my light picked up first a
movement beyond the palaver-house, then as I walked around
it I could see not only two large glowing eyes but the whole
animal almost as clearly as by day. These five-cell electric
shooting lamps are a vast improvement over the old carbide
lamps we used to use and which would never show you more
than the animal's eyes. It was a lioness, and when she turned
broadside-on to look towards me and gave vent to a low
growl, an almost maneless lion followed by another lioness
came from between two huts just beyond her, and also stopped
to gaze towards the light.

The nearer lioness was only about eight or nine yards away,
the others two or three yards beyond her. I shot the nearer one
first, driving my soft-nosed bullet through her shoulder. She
dropped instantly and I knew she was dead. I at once reloaded
that barrel in the hope of getting a quick right-and-left at the
others. At the shot the second lioness had spun around in a
complete circle and then very obligingly stopped and also
stood broadside-on to me. The lion didn't move. I killed the
second lioness in the same way as I killed the first one. At that,
the second shot, the lion loosed a deep growl and sprang
right over the second lioness.

But he only took another long low bound and then, as I had expected he would, he pulled up and looked back to see what was happening and, possibly, why his mates didn't seem to be taking any interest in the proceedings. It was the chance I wanted and had hoped for, and he received the contents of my left barrel immediately behind the left shoulder. Owing to the angle at which he was standing I was unable to put the bullet through the shoulder. This meant that he was able to dash off; but he only went about forty yards and then collapsed. I found afterwards that the bullet had ploughed through the top of his heart and stopped against the inside of the off shoulder. He was dead when I found him lying on the outskirts of the kraal.

The villagers had made no sound whilst the shooting was taking place nor while I was following the lion to where he fell; but I now called out to let them know that three of the maneaters were dead and would not worry them any more. At that they broke into yells of delight and relief, the women ullullulluing in a way that could be heard far and wide. The warning drum would have been heard in every kraal in the district and so, of course, would the shooting. There was no way of preventing the people from the nearer kraals pouring out of their huts to see the dead lions, to see with their own eyes that they were really and truly dead. I hoped, however, that those from the farther kraals would contain themselves in patience until the following morning, because after all I had only shot three of the maneaters. There were known to be at least five in the area, and we had no means of knowing where the others were. However, the people in the more outlying kraals also knew that there were more than three maneaters around, and moreover had no means of knowing how many I had slain with those three shots. They very wisely decided to stay where they were.

There was no further warning or alarm during the rest of the night. The following morning I went out and shot a waterbuck for the headman and his people, and a reedbuck for my lads and myself.

I need scarcely mention that it is essential when shooting right in the centre of a native kraal for the hunter to use bullets of a type and weight that will NOT pass clear through any animal shot, because of the very real danger of the bullet boring through the flimsy walls of the huts and possibly killing or seriously wounding one or more of the occupants.

The shooting of the three lions was an excellent and very encouraging start; but it was only a start. There were still at least two maneaters left. If the three I had shot were part of the bunch of five that had been seen several times I guessed that the two left would prove to be practically if not quite full-grown cubs. All the carnivora, bird as well as animal, keep their young around until they are almost mature, presumably for instruction purposes.

Nothing much happened for the following two or three days, except that I bagged another maneating croc on the same sandbank where I had shot the first one. Here again the contents of its stomach left no doubt about it either. I also again slightly reduced the game population for the benefit of the locals as well as ourselves.

And then one morning two breathless runners arrived from Chimbidzi with word of another kill. As soon as they had swilled out their mouths and then had a long drink of water they sat down and told me all about it.

It seems that an elderly man, having heard of the shooting of the three maneaters at Nsungu, followed by several days of peace, had apparently assumed that the danger was over and relaxed his precautions. Instead of remaining in his hut until after the sun was well up, as he and all others had been doing for the past few months, he had foolishly gone out of his hut at crack of dawn to relieve a call of nature. The other villagers had heard a couple of yells, the second one choked off short and mingling with the deep growl of a lion. There could be no doubt as to what had happened. Africans can be and are very brave when one of their own people is in danger, but they can surely be sympathised with on this occasion for not going to the old man's assistance. Remember, for all practical purposes they were unarmed: their little spears—those who had one—were not much more than ornaments. Like the Englishman's walking stick or the heavy ugly crook stick wealthy Americans carry when attending the opera in New York, the Africans take their spears with them as a matter of habit and not because they are likely to be of the slightest use to them for any conceivable purpose. Their only other weapon was their little tomahawk.

These people had been living under a positive reign of terror for many months, and that is liable to sap any man's courage eventually when he knows that he is just about helpless against the enemy. Also, they had recognised the voice and knew that it belonged to an old man who was just about useless both to himself and everyone else. It was obvious that he was dead when his voice was choked off so abruptly. Was it worth risking their lives to save his dead body? Had these people been Masai they would undoubtedly have sallied forth and might have killed at least one of the lion. Even Masai, and I have an unbounded admiration for those fine fellows, could not have cleared the district of the man-eaters. They would have been able to do little in all that continuous bush and thorn. Elsewhere the conditions were such that it would have been impossible for them to have surrounded the lion in their usual way.

After a little while some of the villagers had emerged from

their huts and could see the hindquarters and tails of two lion on the far side of a clump of bush. The lion were obviously feeding on the body of the old man, but the natives were unable to see if there were more than the two lion. The two runners had immediately been sent off to tell me.

Chimbidzi was ten or twelve miles away. These fellows had run all the way, nevertheless the lion would already have decamped. Even if there were only the two lion, the body of an old man would not detain them long. It seemed the sheerest waste of energy to walk all the way out there. My normal walking speed is three miles an hour and I do not care to increase it much beyond that if I have any distance to cover. At three miles an hour I can keep going all day.

I decided to go because, if I refused this first call, the villagers might become disheartened and fail to let me know whenever the lion were seen or heard, and without that information my hunting would be solely by guess and by God—decidedly a case of a few needles in a very large haystack. I would be unable to plan any strategy or tactics.

Accordingly, with a couple of day's rations for all hands and a light bedding-roll, we set out. Now this was not only maneater country but country in which the maneaters had to a very great extent changed their normal custom and were quite ready to hunt by day. It behoved me to be very much on the alert and also to see to it that none of the party became stragglers. All maneaters, whatever their type, will invariably take that almost inevitable straggler—someone who has stopped for a moment to adjust his load, to tie a sandal, or to relieve nature. If any of my party wanted to stop for any purpose they were to say so and we would all stop and wait. It would be midday or close to it by the time we reached our destination, and on account of the heat I felt pretty sure that all lion throughout the district would be lying-up in whatever shade they could find. Experience has taught me never to take needless risks nor forget my bushcraft.

The thought that kept recurring to me as we walked, just as it had been before and just as it still is, was a never-ending source of wonder and admiration to me how cheerfully and willingly my men would accompany me into known maneater country for the express purpose of hunting those maneaters. They were unarmed yet daily and nightly they were exposing themselves and risking their lives with only my word for it that they would get an additional bonus when I had at last succeeded in removing the scourge. Never once did I have any one of them ask about a bonus before I had mentioned it; never once did I hear a murmur, much less a bellyache, because I was exposing them to very real danger. Naturally, I took every possible precaution to safeguard them. It was well-known that throughout all the years of my wanderings I had never had a single man of mine even hurt much less killed. And then, of course, the African is blessed with that happy philosophy which suggests that unpleasant things never happen to one's self but always to the other man.

When we arrived at Chimbidzi I was taken at once to see all there was to be seen. It was little enough. What was left of the old man could nearly have been tied up in a large handkerchief. One could clearly see where the lion had pounced on him and then carried him away to where he was joined by his companion for the feed: the old chap's heels dragging along the ground had left a trail. But the ground on the far side of the bush—where the lion had fed—was stony and it was impossible to say how many lion there had been there: two certainly, but there may or may not have been others. The body of a man is not very big and the two lion would have had to change their positions from time to time. The only thing left now was to endeavour to spoor them and hope that we would come to some place where the ground would take and hold an impression of the pugs. I could then see how many there were in the party, though I meant to tackle them whether they were few or many if I could contact them.

So after a pot of tea, which he shared with me, my gun-bearer and I set out. The ground being so stony it was very slow work. It was useless attempting to spot each and every pug-mark. No good tracker ever does so—it would be much too slow. One looks ahead and spots some tiny indication: a small loose stone that has recently been moved, a dry stick on which the white ants (termites) have been working and which has obviously been recently disturbed, and just here and there a little depression on a softer piece of ground without stones which might be the toe-print of a man but which is more probably part of a pug-mark. It is a never-ending joy to watch a good tracker at work. But that is his job: the hunter's part is to keep his eyes roving constantly ahead and on both sides to spot the first glimpse of the quarry. What's more, the tracker will do a very much better job of his tracking if he knows that he can rely upon the hunter to keep a close look-out. If both are concentrating on the spoor the hunter will probably fail to see the quarry in time. The animal will be motionless, probably lying down whereas the attacker will be moving.

At long last after we had followed them for nearly a mile, which took close on two hours, we came to a place where there were no stones and where a patch of grass had been burnt off. Here the pug-marks of five lion were very clear. Unfortunately, that was all we did see. Beyond that burnt patch there was a rise in the ground and it was so impossibly stony that, although we searched and searched over a wide area, the lion might have evaporated into thin air for all that we could see to the contrary. So there was nothing for it but to return to camp at Chimbidzi. I was not terribly upset at this setback because it was only what I had expected, knowing this stony area as I did.

On the way back to the village I was lucky enough to spot a kudu which provided us and the villagers with fresh meat. I did not worry about the lion hearing the shot because in all probability they had never heard a rifle shot before and so would not know what it was or even whence the noise came. Even if they followed customary maneater habits they were likely to be several miles away by now and would not be returning here until after they had visited other kraals.

It was this that had me disinclined to rush off to Chimbidzi when the word had come in. I had thought of strolling slowly along the path from Nsungu tonight instead in the hope that I might meet the maneaters coming towards me. But there was no use worrying about that now. I have explained why I did not follow my inclination and am sure I was right to do so, even though it might possibly mean that another kill would take place and I be too far away to do anything about it.

As it transpired, however, it was a good thing that I had come to Chimbidzi. There was another kraal a little distance away from it on the path to Nsungu that I had completely forgotten. I had passed through it on my way to Chimbidzi and it was only then that I remembered it. When I had last been in this district it had only consisted of two or three huts, but I now found that there were a dozen or more.

Early in the night we heard the warning drums coming from there. Evidently the old man they had killed that morning had provided a very inadequate meal for the five, two of which were fully mature and the remainder very nearly so.

Saduko and I set out and followed the path to the neighbouring kraal, which was only about a mile away. As we closed in we could hear shouts in addition to the constant rolling and tapping of the drums and also the snarls of an angry lion and the deep growls of another. The beam of my lamp showed the entire party of five lion clustered about the door of one of the huts. An almost full-grown cub was endeavouring to claw aside the reed door whilst a big lioness, possibly his mother, stood close beside him growling. One of the occupants of the hut was jabbing a spear through the reeds of the door, and even as I brought up my rifle he pricked the young lion with it and was answered by another angry snarl. I killed the big lioness with my first shot and the youngster with my left barrel. My stouthearted gunbearer was right beside me with my second rifle held out all ready for me to grab as he took the empty one from me.

These two quick shots had been fired at a range of about fifteen or sixteen feet, because I had had to turn around the huts to get to the doorway that was being attacked. At the first shot that killed his mother the young lion had merely looked over his shoulder at me. He hadn't otherwise moved, nor, I think did the three survivors until I fired the second shot. But at that one, and whilst I was exchanging rifles, they spun around in all directions as lion so often do. The lion was the closest to me and was somewhat in my line of fire for the second lioness, so I shot him. But now, instead of giving me another easy shot as unsophisticated lion so often do at night, I was surprised and very disappointed when the second lioness whipped around and bounded away between the huts, the second youngster going with her, before I could get my sights on either of them.

I dare say I could have taken a hasty snap-shot at the young one's hindquarters, but I have never indulged in such shooting. I am and always have been a firm believer in never squeezing trigger until I can clearly see my way to either kill or definitely cripple. Besides, from my knowledge of lion and their ways I felt pretty certain that that lioness would come back possibly the following morning early or perhaps next night to look for her mate. A male might not but a female usually will because there are more females than males about and therefore she would not perhaps find it quite so easy to find another mate as would the lion. Be that as it may, I do know that whereas you can never be sure of the male returning after an affair like this, you can be fairly confident that the female will. The only thing that might prevent her doing so would be the fear of possible danger to her cub in spite of the fact that he was practically full-grown.

Naturally, there was great jubilation amongst the villagers both at my arriving so opportunely on the scene and at the knowledge that another three of the maneaters had been slain. I had followed the two that dashed off for a short distance but had failed to pick up their eyes in the beam of my light because the bush and forest around this kraal was rather dense. I warned the villagers to get back into their huts and stay there until I gave them the all clear. I decided to see the night out here in the hope that the two survivors would return later when things had quietened down. The woman and children who had been in the hut that had been attacked moved into another, but the man who had been wielding the spear insisted that he would remain there with me and Saduko.

I told my companions that they could sleep whenever they wanted to, and presently they lay down. I sat on. There had been a young moon but it was very close to the horizon and almost entirely obscured by the trees of the forest before I spotted some movement away on the outskirts of the kraal beyond two other huts. It could have been hyenas sneaking around, but I had a hunch it was the two lion. Although the young moon was so low and the trees throwing shadows, I had quite a good view of things because I had only partially closed the reed door of the hut. I was sitting in darkness whilst by contrast it seemed quite light outside. For a long time nothing further happened. I was tempted to go out and swing the beam of my lamp around, but finally decided against it. I reasoned that if the lioness was coming to look for her mate she would come a lot closer and thus give me an easy shot at close range. If I went out she might spot the beam of my lamp before I spotted her and perhaps go for her life. She would realise now that that dazzling light spelt danger.

Patience is an absolutely essential attribute of the hunter and I am usually very patient. But on this occasion I was too patient. This particular lioness was unduly cautious and did not approach as I had felt so sure she would. The moon was right on the horizon shining through the trunks of the trees where there happened to be a gap in the undergrowth and bush. By its light, I saw two shadows moving off into the forest where I had originally seen them. It was a very long shot for night shooting, but I switched on my lamp so as to see my sights and fired at what seemed to be the larger of the two, the one in front. It seemed probable that the lioness would be leading the way, and I wanted her if possible. There would be a much greater likelihood of the young one then stopping for a moment to see what his mother was doing and so give me a shot at him also. Unfortunately I was wrong. It was the young lion that collected my bullet and the lioness gave me no chance at all. At the shot she bounded right over the young one and disappeared in the bush. I rushed across in case she stopped, but if she did it could only have been momentarily. There was no sign of her when I reached the dead youngster. As there was little or no likelihood of her returning again, Saduko and I made our way back to Chimbidzi to sleep through the rest of the night.

We got away early next morning to return to Nsungu. I was leading the way and we were, of course, proceeding in as compact a party as the narrow footpath would allow since there was at least one maneater left out of this troop and, if all the accounts we had heard were accurate, possibly two more. We were, I suppose, a couple of miles or thereabouts beyond the village where I had shot the four when I suddenly felt uneasy. Up to that time I had been strolling along quite happily, pleased with my success thus far, and feeling glad that the natives throughout the district had carried out my instructions about the burning off of all grass. From our little hill at Nsungu I had been able to see the smoke of the grass-fires in all directions, which shows they had done their work thoroughly.

Without any warning I felt positive there was danger very, very close. I halted, brought my rifle down from my shoulder so as to hold it in two hands at the "ready", slid forward the safety catch, and indicated to my men to close right up. I then began to move very slowly and carefully forward. This sudden warning, which I knew so well, could only mean a maneater: there was no other danger in this district. I have had occasion to refer to this inner premonition before, a premonition which has never let me down, so I will only say here that if you want it to work for you, you must always accept it instantly *and act upon it*. Never attempt to balance it against your reasoning powers.

As I very cautiously moved forward I felt an irresistible urge to keep my eyes more and more to the right. This satisfied me that the danger lay there. It was more than probable too because there was considerable bush and scrub on that side of the path, and it was the most likely side on which to find the maneaters. The left side of the path was very much more open here and ran in undulations towards the range of hills that contained the Gorge. It was all lightly forested with widely-scattered bush. The ground was all stony. As the sense of danger grew stronger I signed to my fellows to leave the path and make their way out over the more open ground to the left of the path. I gradually edged out that way myself because it seemed that the maneater must be ambushing us behind one of the many clumps of bush that grew close to the path on the other side. Were I to continue along the path I might walk literally into her jaws and have no time to do anything. By circling out a bit over the more open ground I should be able to get a shot at her if she attacked or, if she decided not to, possibly get a smack at her before she could get away. That she or another was there I had no possible doubt: I KNEW it.

It was awkward having her there on my right because it meant that I had to sidle along more or less crabwise in order to keep facing as much as possible in the direction from which she would come and so as to be able to bring my rifle to bear with the minimum delay. It is so very seldom that a maneater, will rush its quarry across the open. It much prefers the close approach followed by a quick pounce. I deliberately refrained therefore, from making my own detour more than about fifteen yards from the path. I wanted to tempt the brute to attack since otherwise I might not get a shot on account of the density of the bush where she was.

Another step and I spotted her. She merged so perfectly into her background and surroundings that I might have failed to do so had not a slight movement of her tail caused an equally slight movement of some short grass in which she was crouching between two clumps of bush. As I dropped to one knee, raising my rifle to my shoulder, she decided to come. Doubtless I looked very defenceless kneeling there barely fifteen strides away from her; and then doubtless she was peeved at having her mate and her cub both killed the previous night. And she must have had a very good appetite by now. If she hadn't been hungry she would not have been there right alongside a footpath. Loosing a deep growl, very different from the savage grating roar loosed by a wounded lion that is charging for revenge, she hurled herself at me. As she was only fifteen yards away I fired immediately. My bullet took her in the mouth, shattering her lower jaw, and then driving down her throat into her chest. She came on for one more bound then skidded to her nose, but did not quite fall. She hauled herself to her feet and stood, legs wide apart, head down while she choked and retched. Another shot through the top of her head finished her.

That was eight of the brutes and I realised how very fortunate I had been to bag them so soon after arriving in the district. I knew only too well how many weeks it might have taken me, and how many it had taken me on previous occasions elsewhere. The question now was: Were there any more and if so, how many? I rather doubted that there could be any left. This was by no means a densely-populated area. In fact, I was surprised that it had held so many maneaters. What between lion and croc the native population must have been very considerably reduced during the past eight or nine months.

I remained on at Nsungu for another ten days, killing three more big crocs; and then, as no further word had come in of attacks by lion or even of their being seen, I left the district.

E

The Makossa Marauders

I HAD been sent for to deal with a very bad elephant herd. It was a pretty large herd of somewhere between sixty and eighty head—the bush and forest was generally so close that it was quite impossible to form more than a very approximate idea of their numbers. Not only did they, year after year, cause absolute devastation to the local natives' food crops amounting to considerably more than partial starvation, but they had become extremely vicious and deadly. When the unfortunate natives tried to drive them out of the lands and save even a little of the year's food supply, the elephant would attack and chase the natives, killing any of whom they were able to catch. The herd seemed to be led by a big old cow.

Two native hunters who had been supplied with worn-out old rifles by somebody had been killed and another seriously injured by this herd; one half-breed hunter had been killed; and two or three white hunters had been very badly frightened as also had another half-breed. I rather think that yet another white hunter had been killed by them. Their reputation could scarcely have been worse.

But where elephant needed no encouragement to become crop-raiders, I have no hesitation in blaming the pseudo hunters through pricking and wounding many members of the herd, making them vicious and turning them, or at any rate some of them, into man-killers. It has been my experience throughout that whenever a herd of elephant turns nasty it is the result of being constantly chivvied about and wounded by excitable inexperienced men, probably armed with totally unsuitable weapons. Many elephant herds raid crops. When the villagers who, if they know they are liable to be raided, sleep out in the lands on high roofed-platforms among the crops, beat drums, shout and yell, and rattle stones in tin cans, the elephant usually move off and look for some other place where there is less noise to disturb them. They are not in the least likely to attack. Elephant are very intelligent and know perfectly well when they are doing wrong. One has only to see how, after raiding in a district wherein they know they are likely to be followed-up and punished, they will twist and turn and deliberately take the most difficult way to wherever they intend to spend the hot midday hours. It is obvious that they are hoping to shake off the pursuit.

It has been found that the best way in which to drive home the lesson that it is inadvisable to raid is to shoot them when actually raiding. Elephant will give that place a wide berth in future. However, it is not too satisfactory to tackle them when actually in the crops if there are many of them, because the millet—and most of these crops are millet—stands from twelve to fifteen feet in height. It is, therefore, seldom possible to shoot more than perhaps a couple of them. One cannot see the others, at any rate not sufficiently clearly to place an accurate shot. The killing of one or two will probably only have the effect of driving the herd a mile or so away to some other unfortunate's crop. In the case of a big herd it is necessary to shoot a number of them. Accordingly, one has to pick up their spoor in the morning and follow them to where they halt for their midday rest.

Some of the worst herds I have encountered have been, like this one was, led by one or two old cows. And the reason for this, and why they sometimes become so vicious and fearless of man, is because the elephant-hunting that has ever taken place in Portuguese East Africa has usually been for ivory.

The ivory-hunter does not shoot cows because their tusks are scarcely worth powder and shot. Cow ivory is used for making billiard balls (it is preferred for them on account of its closer grain—the balls won't warp so readily), but not much of cow ivory is required at any time. Old cows often enjoy complete immunity all their lives and sometimes become positively contemptuous of Man and his works. They can be very dangerous, especially when they assume leadership of some herd.

I camped down near a kraal which seemed to be roughly in the centre of the devastated area. I had arrived in the afternoon, so after the usual pot of tea I had some of the locals take me around to see some of the damage. It surpassed anything I have ever seen, and I have seen plenty of damage done by elephant. It was a fairly extensive area with wide-spreading acres of millet. The people had been forced to plant far more than they needed under normal conditions because they knew that the elephant would eat, destroy and trample down, most of it. The natives told me that no other hunter had come near them for a couple of years now, so bad a reputation had these elephant earned. It was a fertile district and these people had been here for generations. Naturally, they didn't want to have to migrate elsewhere. It was extremely improbable that they would be able to find another area equally fertile nowadays, and few people like having to pack up and move house and home to some strange place. In the case of the natives it would mean that the menfolk would have to go first in order to clear forest and bush and commence building operations. The women and children, and perhaps just a few of the older men, would have to remain to guard the crops and eventually harvest what the elephant had left behind. They would also have to prepare meals for their menfolk who would send back for it from time to time; then finally all would have to help carry the harvest to the new home, and as soon as they got there commence breaking the ground for next year's crops. A big undertaking.

It might be asked why these poor people were left for a couple of years without anyone coming to help them. The answer is that others who were hunting in the territory were not interested since they worked to collect as much ivory as they could. Marauders often carry worthwhile ivory, but mixed herds usually consist of cows, calves, immature bulls, and a few herd bulls as breeding animals. It is seldom nowadays that one finds a really heavy-tusked bull with the herd. Even in bygone days the big old bulls, when they lost interest in the cows, used to wander off by themselves or with an elderly companion or two, and live a bachelor existence thenceforth.

I was inundated with calls for help from all sides. If that season I happened to be working some districts, perhaps a couple of hundred miles away, I could scarcely abandon the natives up there to help others. The most I could do was to shoot-up as many raiding parties as I could throughout any given district one season, and then hope that they would learn their lesson and leave these people alone next year. Of course, there would always be a few lone raiders and an occasional small party, but the natives could cope with them if only by planting a bit more than they otherwise would have done.

As usual word whipped around the district that I was there I was not surprised, therefore, when a runner arrived early next morning to tell me that elephant had been raiding one of the outlying kraals during the night. I had already had breakfast, so out I went. We picked up the spoor of a small party and proceeded to follow them. They seemed to be all mature animals although there was nothing very big amongst them. It could be a party that usually lived together, on the other hand they might have broken away from the big herd for a day or two. This is by no means unusual. A large herd of elephant is not just a conglomerate body of elephant: it consists of numerous family parties, each of which will have its own leader. There will then be one or at the most two elderly beasts, quite possibly not belonging to any of the families, who will be accepted as leader or joint leaders of the herd. This can be very clearly seen when you open fire on a large herd in fairly open country and kill the leader with your first shot right there where he stands. The remainder of the herd do not know he is dead and, splitting up into their family groups, they stand around awaiting some signal from the big leader. The individual family leaders will not usually attempt to move off. It is this that makes it possible to kill a number of the herd if you have dropped the main leader or leaders with clean brain-shots at the commencement of the operation. And that, of course, is what one always tries to do. It enables one to impress such a severe lesson upon the survivors that they may not have to be shot-up again for years.

The party I was following had sampled the millet in several different places and then wandered off and drifted around seemingly aimlessly in the strange way elephant often will. They stop for a short while here and there: tear a branch or two off some tree to get at the inner bark, which they are very fond of; they pause at a clump of bamboo and eat some of that; they push down or snap off, six or eight feet above the ground, another tree for the sake of a trunk full of the upper leaves or a few small wild fruit. They are most destructive things. The following of a small party of elephant is slow and difficult work when they are wandering around some area where they have been feeding daily for weeks or even months. Today's spoor is underlaid by yesterday's and that of the day before. At this season of the year the ground and trampled-down grass is dry and does not easily distinguish between tracks only a few hours old from those only a few hours older.

The droppings are a good indication; but they can also be deceptive if taken on their own. Those of yesterday which have been lying in the shade may appear fresher than those of today which have been lying in the sun, especially as the hours roll by.

We followed, hour after hour, Saduko and two local trackers puzzling out today's tracks from the maze of tracks we found everywhere. The elephant in this district were resident here: they did not indulge in those seasonal migrations one found in various other parts. Presumably they found all they wanted to eat here throughout the year.

After about four hours on the spoor we heard unmistakable elephant noises on our half-left front. As the breeze was favourable, I made straight for them. It was now getting along towards midday, and I knew that the wind was apt to become fitful, blowing from all points of the compass in rapid succession, for an hour or so around midday. So I wanted to get busy amongst this party whilst it was still steady.

There were seven of them, mostly standing around doing nothing. There was one bull somewhat bigger than the rest of them. He was probably their leader although he did not seem to be carrying more than about forty pounds of ivory in each of his tusks. One of the other bulls was only a little smaller. The remainder were cows and younger bulls. But that was more or less what I expected from their spoor. Most herd bulls, that is, breeding bulls, usually carry between thirty and forty pounds of ivory a side.

I walked up to within about twenty-five paces of them and opened fire. My first two quick shots dropped the two larger bulls, and I immediately exchanged rifles. In view of the fact that these elephant had not been shot at for a couple of years or more, the two crashing reports of my powerful elephant rifle coming rapidly on the heels of one another and without any warning that there was a man within a thousand square miles of them, must have given these elephant a considerable shock. For a moment they did not seem to believe their ears. They threw their trunks up over their heads, swung out their great ears until they stood at right-angles to the head, and swung around to face in all directions. Before they had made up their minds as to what they were going to do about it, I had dropped two more of them. Since I had made a point of shooting the older ones each time, this left only the three younger bulls. I might or might not have killed them all; but they took the decision out of my hands by wheeling around and going for their lives. I believe I could have killed at least one if not two of them as they ran; but I did not fire. I had slain four of the party, and if they had been a temporary break away from the big herd, well—I'd be tackling them some day.

We removed the tails in the customary manner and returned to camp. The two local trackers told me that most of the elephant which frequented this district spent a lot of time in an impossible piece of forest. The trees were big and tall and the branches mostly met overhead; yet in spite of that there was the most indescribable undergrowth. It was utterly impenetrable except along the tracks beaten out by the elephant themselves; but although one could force one's way along like that, one could only see a matter of a very few feet in any direction on account of the huge leaves that covered this undergrowth and which were evergreen. Moreover, this stuff, which wasn't thorn, would fall into place again behind either man or elephant just like a curtain. In spite of the fact that elephant had been spending a lot of time in there ever since these men could remember and possibly ever since the world began, yet there was no sign of wear on these leaves. The natives told me that several genuine hunters had tried to get a shot in there in bygone days, but all had had to give it best and admit defeat. For many years now nobody had attempted it. I asked them if they had ever been through the forest. They had never been right through, nor, so far as they knew, had anyone else. It certainly sounded very different from any forest I had ever been in; and I wondered if perhaps were there not open spaces right away in the centre of it, as there nearly always are somewhere in African forests. I thought that if I could penetrate to such an open space I might be able to make a real killing, as I had done elsewhere on different occasions.

Nothing happened for several days after this, and I remember thinking to myself that it was a good thing that elephant did not raid the crops every night. Hardly any animal is so fond of a mixed diet as elephant are, which is probably why they did not return.

The locals were now afraid to sleep in their lands or attempt to drive the elephant out when they came raiding. Several had been killed last year and two more this year. After that the natives just made no attempt to do anything about it. After all, what could they do?

I did not go out looking for the elephant. It is usually sheer waste of time and energy to do so. If you want to find raiders, it is best just to wait for them to come and then get out after them.

With nobody sleeping in the lands it would be quite possible for even a large herd to come raiding without anyone being the wiser until next morning, because elephant can and frequently do come on these raids, eat their fill, and be off again without making a sound of any sort. It has been known on many occasions for natives to be sleeping in their lands, right in the centre of the crops being raided, and not know a thing about it until they awoke in the morning and saw the damage. It is clear that those elephant knew perfectly well they were doing wrong, because under normal conditions the herds are noisy if there are calves amongst them.

However, the big herd in this district were so contemptuous of Man that they made no secret of their advent when they came: cows trumpeted and calves screamed and yelled, so that they could be heard half a mile or more away. It was several nights after I had shot-up that other party that I awoke and heard them. Saduko had also awakened, so we sallied forth. The moon was waning and had not yet risen. I was glad of that because the herd was to the east of me and had the moon been up it would have been a nuisance more or less in front of me, and would have rendered my lamp less effective.

Although it was a big herd and I wanted the leaders and as many as possible of the others, I decided on this night assault, both because it would lessen the damage they would do and also because it would show the survivors of the assault that they could expect in future a very different reception from the feeble attacks they had hitherto met. I wanted to show them that they were not going to have it all their own way. I did not expect a very big bag tonight; but that would not matter because I would most certainly get after them on the next day.

We found them about a quarter of a mile away. They had emerged from the forest to the south which formed the boundary of the lands. We made our way along the strip of land between the forest and the cultivated ground where the walking was easier. And once again I had to marvel at the African's night vision. It far surpasses that of any white man I have ever met. Had I been alone I would have been tripping and stumbling over things and falling into holes; but with Saduko in the lead I didn't even stub a toe on anything. He seemingly had no difficulty in seeing these things, and would merely indicate their presence by smacking his hand lightly against his bare thigh and then pointing a slender black finger down behind him as he avoided some obstacle.

The herd had spread out through the millet, trampling down

ten times as much as they ate. I continued to advance until I was almost abreast of them. This had me across-wind from them. I could not advance very well across the trampled down millet stalks. The going would be altogether too rough and it would be too dangerous to change position, since there would be the risk of falling or tripping. The herd being so bad-tempered I did not mean to take any risks. There were plenty of elephant within easy range, but before switching my light towards them, I first sent the beam into the forest just in case there happened to be an old cow there. I did not want to have her make a sudden and absolutely silent attack from behind me, as elephant sometimes will. Up to this time I had not had the lamp switched on. However, there was nothing lurking in the forest, so I swung the beam around towards the nearest members of the herd.

Except that I did not want to shoot calves if I could possibly avoid it, I did not care what they were: bulls or cows, young or old. It would be necessary to shoot a number out of this herd if the lesson was to be effective, and I could not hope to bag a sufficient number of elderly beasts. Besides, the local natives badly needed meat and plenty of it. They would eat a lot and then smoke the remainder and carry it away and barter it for grain to replace what the elephant had destroyed. I could see on all sides the surface indications of serious and prolonged malnutrition, especially on the women and children.

My first two shots brought down the two nearest elephant, and I quickly exchanged rifles. There was absolute complete silence after the shots and whilst I made the exchange. The herd all stood there like statues or like a child's toys from a Noah's Ark. My next two shots dropped another two. As I took over the rifle which Saduko had reloaded for me, pande- monium broke out. Not only had those shots told them it was not thunder they had heard, they disclosed my whereabouts.

(When a rifle is fired unexpectedly and at fairly close quarters it is often extremely difficult to locate the source of the noise.)

Cows trumpeted shrilly as they commenced to drive their calves ahead of them out of the lands and into the forest and there was a general surge in the direction of the forest by the main body of the herd. Away on the far side of the herd, and completely concealed both by them and by the long fifteen-foot millet, I could hear several short but very loud trumpet-blasts, repeated in rapid succession. I guessed the old cow who acted as leader was responsible for them. The blasts continued and from the movements in the millet it looked as though she was trying to charge towards me. However, the cluster of animals between us must have interfered with her intention.

I bagged another two as a grey mass of elephant, heading for the forest, rushed past me, and then shot two more when there seemed to be a pause. This took place when the old cow halted on finding her way blocked by a dense clump of others. The survivors wheeled partially away from me and quickly disappeared. I did not see the old cow at all nor any of the bigger bulls. They must have been away at the head of the herd with the old cow.

I was quite satisfied with my night's work. I doubted very much that the elephant would return to the crops tonight. But that old cow would be very angry at my daring to shoot-up her precious herd and would probably be nursing considerable frustration at being unable to get to me.

This night's experience was further corroboration of what my previous experience with so-called mass-mankilling herds had shown me: that these so-called mass attacks are not so at all. Invariably I had found that there were just the one, or possibly two, bad beasts—be they elephant or buffalo. Shoot them and the danger disappears. The remainder of the herd will show a proper and healthy respect for Man. Had that old cow been on my side of the herd when I opened fire, she would almost certainly have charged and quite possibly the others would have come with her; but since she could not reach me, without her leadership the others proved entirely innoxious. But it would be very necessary to kill her: she was definitely dangerous. Whether or not there were any others like her only time would tell.

We returned to camp. The villagers had, of course, heard the shooting and the trumpeting of the herd. There were numbers of them around my camp waiting to see if either of us would return. They had recognised the trumpet-blasts of the old cow —the man-killer—and felt sure that both of us would be torn in pieces or trampled into the ground. They told me that that was the old cow's war cry which she invariably loosed when killing or when about to kill. They could scarcely credit their own eyes when we threw down the tails of the slain: they had to handle them to be sure that their eyes were not deceiving them. They looked with awe and admiration towards my stout-hearted gunbearer who had actually been present reloading my rifles for me whilst no less than eight of this man-killing herd had been shot! And at night, too!

I persuaded the natives to go at last, telling them that we wanted to get some sleep so that we could get after the herd as soon as it was light enough to see the elephant spoor.

At crack of dawn, Saduko and I had breakfast and then started out with the two trackers to pick up the spoor of the herd just as soon as it was light enough to see it. As I expected, the herd had decamped but they had not stampeded with the usual blind rush. They had for about fifty yards or so, after which they had dropped to a fast walk and gradually assumed line-ahead. For the first couple of hours spooring was easy and we followed as fast as we could comfortably walk; but then the herd had commenced twisting and turning, feeding here and there, and then moving on. Even with a big herd like this the trackers occasionally had to puzzle out which was the freshest lot of tracks where there were so many of yesterday's underlying them. The herd had been wandering around this same area the previous day, quite possibly during the evening before coming to the lands. But they were excellent trackers and were seldom long at fault.

Eventually, the herd started off in a more or less straight line to the south-east and the trackers halted and shook their heads. I asked them what was the matter. They told me that there was no question but that the herd was making for that impossible forest they had told me about. It would be sheer waste of energy to follow them any further.

Nevertheless, I determined to have a look at it. I told them I wanted to see for myself just what it was like. They were good fellows and put forward no further objections. My successes so far had shown them that I knew my job and would not let them down if things turned nasty. One can fully sympathise with these unarmed men who accompany in-experienced hunters into tight spots never knowing when the pseudo hunter will throw his rifle away and take to his heels. It has happened far too many times. My experience has been that provided you show your men that you can be relied upon, you will have no reason to complain about their staunchness.

After about another hour's tracking, which was merely a case of walking along a clearly defined track and just watching that the herd did not branch off from it, I saw heavy forest stretching right across in front of us. The elephant path we were following led straight towards it. As we closed in I could see that it appeared to be just as described by the two trackers. It was by far the biggest and densest type of forest I had seen anywhere in the Zambezi valley. By big, I refer to the height of the trees which were all big. They towered up with few or no branches for the first twenty or thirty feet, except in the case of some of them which looked as though they had divided into two or occasionally three mighty boles from close to the ground or perhaps ten feet above it. But everywhere between these great monarchs stood the undergrowth. I don't know to this day what it consisted of—I have never before or since seen anything quite like it—but it stood from ten to fifteen feet high and was a mass of large fleshy dark green leaves which grew right down to within about eighteen inches of the ground. And there were no gaps in it. The well-beaten elephant path we had been following seemed to stop abruptly right against this dense evergreen hedge.

Since the elephant had obviously just brushed their way in, I did likewise. But it was a lot easier for them than it was for me. It wasn't merely a hedge: it continued right along and seemingly everywhere. But I continued to follow the track the herd had taken for a while. I quickly realised why our trackers had tried to dissuade me.

The soil of the forest consisted of heavy black clay, or rather greyish-black now that it was dry, and everywhere innumerable large rocks and boulders were embedded in it. During the rains it would have been desperately slippery and treacherous, but in the dry weather it was not so difficult. The density of the undergrowth and the fact that the tops of the great trees mostly met overhead, however, prevented more than an occasional shaft of sunlight penetrating to the ground. So the ground was still somewhat moist and therefore slippery for my rubber-shod shoes. The main trouble was that those big fleshy leaves overhung the track so that one could neither see where one was placing one's foot nor see the spoor. To track the herd in here it would be necessary to have a stick or a light spear with which to push aside the leaves the entire time. And there was not only the one elephant path or track to follow. When out of curiosity I pushed leaves aside, both to my right and to my left, I could see where elephant had passed there also. The massive bushes that comprised the undergrowth were growing perhaps ten or twelve feet apart, and their branches and leaves filled up the gaps between them. This meant that the elephant could drift around in any direction and did not have to keep to their own tracks, as was the case in dense matted thorn bush.

Visibility was merely a courtesy term. One could seldom see more than arm's length in any direction. But just occasionally, very occasionally, when one came to a small watercourse, the ground would dip down to it and thus one got a slightly longer view. It was then possible to see across to the opposite side of the little stream, perhaps ten or a dozen yards, and perhaps the same distance or less in one or other, or even both, directions: up or down stream.

We battled along slowly. I let the trackers take the lead, since that was their job and they both carried a light spear. I felt confident that we would hear the elephant long before we bumped our noses into them. And that is not merely a figure of speech. If an elephant happened to be dozing it would be quite possible to stub one's toes on him under such conditions. But if there were many of them—and we were following a large herd—there would be sure to be various noises which we could identify.

I do not know what the elephant wanted in here. There was no evidence of their feeding off the undergrowth, whilst the trees were much too big for even African elephant to push down and there were no branches they could reach. I suspected they must have come to consider it a sanctuary wherein they would be quite safe. Another attraction would be that it was always cool in there, with no flies to worry them. And they could have a drink of clear cool water whenever they wanted

(*Above*) A troop of bull elephant. Note the tuskless bull; such animals are bad-tempered and very dangerous—potential man-killers.

(*Below*) Elephant are seldom seen enjoying themselves like this in broad daylight nowadays except in reserves and National Parks.

I have often been accused of exaggeration when describing elephant whose tusks reach the ground when the head is held normally. This photograph should refute such criticism.

Sunbathing.

Feeling the heat where shade is sparse.

Potential maneaters, even though they have cubs and are in their prime. Note the spots and markings, not only on cubs but also on adults (but not so distinct on the latter). The "spotted" lion is not a distinct species.

(*Left*) Water carriers.

(*Below*) Typical African river scene. Note the dugout canoe.

An everyday African domestic scene. These are the humble folk who are so often the victims of maneating lion and marauding elephant.

Reach for it, brother! If he fails to get it he will think nothing of pushing the entire tree over, and then possibly turn up his nose at it!

it, as there appeared to be several of these little streams in this part of the forest.

It must have been an hour and a half or more after we entered the forest that we heard the first sound. The silence had been complete. There did not seem to be a solitary bird or beast, which was very unusual. The silence was oppressive: it seemed to weigh down on one. And then there came a deep sigh followed by the loud "clop" as an elephant's ears flopped back against his shoulders. It was impossible to say just how far ahead they were, but since we had heard the sigh they must be close. Not a breath of air stirred here in this great forest and with all that tall dense undergrowth everywhere. We heard the deep shuddering rumble caused by the gases in some unsuspicious elephant's stomach or intestines, and I was surprised we had not heard it long ago. The very dense undergrowth may have deadened noises and prevented them from carrying far. It is impossible to say.

We had only about thirty yards further to go before I realised we had elephant on both sides of us as well as in front. They were close, very close. Yet I could not get even so much as a glimpse of one until I lay down flat on my belly and looked along the ground. It was fairly clear for about a foot or fifteen inches up from the ground, and I could now see elephant's feet in all directions wherever I looked except behind us. I realised how it was we had not heard any noises until we were almost upon them: the elephant were dozing and sleeping. I had expected them, or at least some of them to be feeding, tearing branches off trees and so on, as some of every herd are usually doing. I had not allowed for the fact that there simply was no feed for elephant in the forest.

I manœuvred around as much as possible to see if I could get a shot from some other direction, but it was quite hopeless. Perhaps it was just as well. It is improbable that I could have

shot more than one at the most. That would not have satisfied
me and the old cow would almost certainly have charged the
sound of the shot. In this impossible undergrowth I should
have been in a dangerous situation: I could not have seen her
until she was literally on top of me or my men.

I could not see my men. The undergrowth completely hid
them, except for Saduko who, as a matter of course, kept
right on my heels. But if the two trackers happened to be
attacked, I would be unable to help them. As it did not look
as though the herd had any intention of moving, we withdrew
and returned to camp. There was nothing else we could do
without taking too great a risk. It would now be a matter of
waiting for another chance and hoping to contact the herd
elsewhere than in this maze.

I wondered if the herd always spent the midday hours in
here. My trackers did not know, but they did not think so.
They thought the elephant only rushed in here after being
shot-up, though without doubt they would sometimes go in
for the sake of the cool shade in the hotter weather. In fact it
was quite clear that they must do so, because we had seen spoor
other than that of this morning, and the elephant hadn't been
shot-up for more than two years. The party I had tackled a
few days previously may or may not have belonged to the
big herd and anyway they had been well separated from it.

Getting bored sitting around doing nothing, apart from
bagging a couple of kudu for the pots, I decided to take a
reconnaissance prowl and see if I could not cross the spoor of
the herd. They must have emerged from the forest to feed
and, though there had been no word of their raiding, they
must be somewhere in the district.

So I sent for our two trackers, who knew the district well,
and told them what I had in mind. They were agreeable, so out
we went. They knew all the favoured feeding places for ele-

phant, but as there were many of them, they suggested we
prowl along the edge of the forest. We would then see where
the herd had left it and, if they had returned, how long since
they had done so.

We found where they had left the sanctuary, probably on
the evening of the day we had been in there. Further along,
we found where they had gone in again, possibly yesterday.
But it wasn't until we had covered another mile and a half that
we found what we had been hoping for: their tracks where
they had left the forest this morning.

We followed them for three or four hours. They were
feeding along, stopping here and there, and then moving on
again in the seemingly aimless way elephant do. At last I
spotted them in what might be described as open forest and
bush country, with plenty of grass varying from five to seven
feet long. By no means difficult country in which to hunt
elephant if you can be satisfied with one or two; but I wanted
considerably more than a mere brace. Above all, I wanted that
old cow who acted as leader. The breeze was steady and the
approach was easy but, as is so often the case with these mixed
herds, some of the young elephant standing anything from
seven to nine feet at the shoulder—much the size of the average
Asiatic elephant—would persist in wandering around. There
was always the possibility of one of them getting our wind by
wandering around behind us. If they did, they would almost
certainly give the alarm.

The herd was considerably scattered. I could only see about
a couple of dozen of them at all clearly; but I could pick out
dark shapes here and there in the grass and bits protruding
from behind clumps of bush. I had little doubt that the old
cow would charge instantly when I opened fire. That was
what I wanted because I could not identify her among the
herd. Most of the cows in view had calves of various sizes

with them; but I guessed that the old leader would be past the breeding stage.

I picked out the best bull I could see and another not quite so good standing close to him, and dropped them both with two quick shots. Quickly taking over my second rifle I waited. There was a tremendous commotion now: trumpeting and screaming and a general surging about of the herd, and somewhere beyond I could distinguish quite readily the characteristic series of trumpet-blasts loosed by the old cow.

And then I heard a series of deep throaty roars rapidly approaching. You can never mistake that sound if you have ever heard it: the roars of a charging bull elephant that really means business. It is a tremendous volume of sound, pregnant with meaning. The elephant was coming from a patch of long grass on my half-right front. I turned to face it. At that instant a big bull burst through. With his trunk curled up under his chin and his great ears swung out till they stood at right-angles to his head, possibly fifteen feet across from tip to tip so that he looked like a square-rigger under full sail in the days of wind-jammers, made straight for me. He was only about fifteen paces away when I got a clear view of him. I shot him instantly. He collapsed on his nose and his momentum caused his great tusks to skid along the ground like the runners of a sleigh. All four feet were pointing to the rear, though I did not have time just then to see that.

The old cow was coming, too. She was coming from my half-left front as I faced the fallen bull. As there was only one shot left in my rifle, I exchanged it for the loaded one as I turned to face towards those vicious trumpet-blasts which were rapidly approaching. There was a patch of grass still standing about fifty or sixty yards away, all that in between having been well trampled down. I had thus a clear view and a clear field of fire. And then I saw her—the old leader. She surged through the grass and other members of the herd like a battle-cruiser under maximum power. Immediately behind her came a dense phalanx of massive grey bodies. The others through which she had barged now swung around and joined the mob. With her ears back the cow looked incredibly vicious. I waited until she was about thirty yards away and then took the frontal brain-shot. She was dead before she hit the ground.

With one exception the others stopped when they saw their leader drop right in front of them. The exception was another big cow. She paused, but didn't quite stop. It looked as though she would have liked to press home the charge but needed the moral support of her sister. She came two or three paces closer to me. I think she would have stopped altogether, but I did not give her time to make up her mind either way. I killed her at once. Taking over my loaded rifle I got to work on the rest of the herd. I fired and exchanged rifles with Saduko just as fast as he could reload for me. Without their leaders the remainder of the herd were completely bewildered. They split up into the usual family groups and just stood around not knowing what to do. I went around from group to group, shooting the best of them—which means the leader of each group—and as many more as I deemed desirable depending on how many there were in the particular group. I hoped to dissuade that herd from raiding for many a long day.

It was interesting to see how, when the bull charged, he came alone; but that when the cow came she was accompanied by the remainder of the herd. She had evidently been accepted as the leader. This is not the only herd I have known led by an old cow even although there was an old bull there too. I think perhaps it could be explained by the fact that the older bulls sometimes leave the herd for periods. They either get tired of the cows and the noisy youngsters and, or just feel like a bachelor dander around, whereas the cows remain with the herd always.

It will also have been noted that although the rest of the herd came with the cow when she charged, they were not charging—they were just coming along to see the fun, as it were. Although it all looked most awe-inspiring, not to say terrifying, to see that big mob of elephant come surging straight for one, I KNEW that they would halt as soon as I slew the leader, or, at most, two leaders. But I certainly did not blame our two trackers for beating it for distant parts when they saw that massive phalanx bearing down on us at speed. They had stood by apparently quite contentedly while I shot the charging bull—I had seen out of the corner of my eye that they were still there as I exchanged rifles and turned to face the approaching cow. The attack of the old cow, however, had been too much for them. After all, they well-knew the deadly reputation of the leader; and did not know, as I knew from past experience, that the rest of the herd would halt when she was down. Although they had seen me in action, and knew my reputation, this was something quite different.

They told us later that they had halted when the old cow's trumpet-blasts had stopped instantly on the heels of my shot, and had then crept carefully back to see what on earth was happening when the shooting continued for so long. They were a little shamefaced; but I jollied them and assured them they had no need to be ashamed of themselves, and that neither Saduko nor I would ever mention it to anyone.

I was mightily proud of my faithful Saduko and the staunch way in which he had stood by me, reloading as calmly as though I was shooting wild duck or geese.

The Maiembi Maneater

I HAD a very pleasant base camp at one period on a small island, the only one, in the angle formed by the L of the lake or lagoon of Lifumba. As the crow flies I was, I suppose, about a mile and a half or thereabouts from the river (Zambezi). There was a large sandy island lying offshore there carrying a considerable native population. They were permanent residents there because the river only came over the island during exceptional floods. As on all Zambezi islands which are not covered annually by the seasonal floods, there were large patches of the cane-like *matetti* which grows to a height of twelve to fifteen feet or more. The leaves are pointed, the points being as hard and as sharp as needles.

The people here grow good crops every year on the rich alluvial mud left by the river when the seasonal floods subside, and whilst they are actually subsiding. They also have a few goats and quite a few hogs and live a very pleasant carefree existence. There are no mosquitoes because there is always a fairly swift current in the river and because, on account of the sandy ground, no water lies around. The tsetse fly which swarms on the mainland does not come over here as there is no bush or grass for it. On top of all that, it never gets cold.

From time to time lion swim or paddle across, depending on the depth of water, and take toll of the goats and, above all the pigs. But up to this time they had never interfered with the human inhabitants of the island. The lion might spend a few days, possibly even a week, on the island; and then when the owners close-herded their precious hogs so that the lion were unable to get a feed, the intruders returned whence they came.

Unfortunately, a certain Chefe de Poste from over the river, who had no jurisdiction on the north bank or on this island which lay off the north bank, heard of these occasional visits by lion to this island and decided he wanted to get a good close-up photo of a real wild lion. He sent one of his native police across to the headman of the island with orders that the headman was to send a message across immediately a lion showed up on the island.

Well, the Chefe de Poste was white and he was a government official. Although in those days it was a different government to that on the north bank; the headman did not dare to refuse a representative of authority.

When the next lion came over and grabbed a hog, the headman sent a couple of men across the river by canoe to tell the Chefe. An hour or two later the official arrived and asked to be taken to where the lion was known to be feeding. The beast was easily followed on that clean white sand, but by the time they got to where he had had his feed they found that he had finished and had made his way into a dense tall stretch of *matetti*. He would certainly lie-up there during the day, as the *matetti* would afford cool shade and no likelihood of being disturbed.

The Chefe had brought a powerful lion-trap with him weighing about eighty pounds. He had his men set this where the lion had fed in a little clear space on the edge of the *matetti*. As there was so little left of the hog, he told the headman to provide another—which he promised to pay for—and tie it securely near the trap but on the side near the village. He hoped that the lion would come out of the *matetti* at the same place where he entered, searching to see if he had left himself anything to eat. If the lion did so, perhaps he would step into the trap. The Chefe then went back home, saying he would return next morning. If the lion were caught in the trap, they were not to do anything that might cause the beast to tear off his foot and escape. This often happens with these powerful steel traps.

Sure enough, that night early there came a sudden savage roar followed by a series of roars and snarls in the direction of the trap. It was evident that the wretched lion had stepped into the thing when he made a pounce on the hog which had been tied up there. Early next morning the villagers trooped along to see what there was to be seen. The lion was there all right and tried to make a rush at them; but the trap had been pegged down so firmly that he only came to the length of the chain. The headman drove the people back to the village to await the white man. He knew that the lion would be able to pull the trap adrift without too much difficulty on account of the sandy ground not giving too firm a hold on to the peg.

Messengers were sent across the river again; and an hour or two later the Chefe arrived armed with camera and rifle and accompanied by two native police armed with worn-out old military rifles. The party made its way to where the lion was held. But when the Chefe approached to take a photo the lion made a rush, loosing a savage roar. The Chefe fell over backwards and his contingent legged it in the opposite direction as fast as they could. The photographer scrambled to his feet leaving his camera there, and also departed. The lion had again been pulled up by the chain and was lying down growling and snarling. The jaws of the trap would have broken the lion's foreleg (he had been caught by the off fore) three or four inches above the paw, and if too much twisting and turning took place the paw would be torn off or the lion might even chew it off himself. These traps are cruel and brutal things and ought never to be used, except possibly in the case of maneaters and cattle-killers. Naturally, any means are legitimate to catch them. But this lion was not yet a maneater.

After a while the Chefe pulled himself together and decided that, since the lion seemed to be fairly secure, he must get his camera. But he didn't feel like getting it himself, so told one of his police to get it while he covered the man with his rifle. The policeman handed his old rifle to his companion and advanced towards the lion. But before he reached the camera the lion made another jump towards him, roaring savagely. At that, the white man fired his rifle at the lion but was so excited and scared that he only slightly wounded him. The lion thereupon reared up on his hind legs, waving the eighty-pound trap in the air, and loosed such a shattering roar, that the "hunt" was completely demoralised. They withdrew and the Chefe considered it was time he had some refreshment. He broached some sardines and bread, and had a glass or two of wine. After that, he thought he would shoot the lion and *then* take his photos. He stalked up very carefully to where he thought he ought to be able to see his quarry, flanked on either side by his rifle-armed police. To his chagrin—and possibly to his relief!—he found that the lion had departed minus one paw which was still in the trap.

The Chefe cleared off in his canoe across the river where there was no chance of the lion getting to him. He was leaving a crippled and savagely vindictive lion behind him on a thickly populated island where there was no game, and even if there had been, the lion with his missing paw would have been unable to catch and kill it for some considerable time. That, however, did not cause the Chefe to lose a wink of sleep, though the lion was almost certain to become a maneater as soon as he became really hungry.

For five days the lion lay up nursing his wounds. Then hunger drove him out. In the meantime, since there had been neither sight nor sound of the lion, the natives being what they are either forgot all about him or else assumed he had made his way back to the mainland. Had they taken the trouble to stroll along the north shore of the island they would have failed to see his spoor and therefore would have known that he must still be on the island.

The first they knew was when they heard a savage roar right on the outskirts of the main village or kraal one night. Although they would shut up their hogs if it was known that there were lion on the island, the villagers did not usually bother to do so. Moreover, they themselves slept in the open unless it was raining and anyway the reed doors of their huts were not fastened in any way: they merely propped a stick against them. As the moon was full they were able to see the lion as he killed and carried off a small hog. Lion do not roar as they kill. The reason this one did was probably because in the excitement of securing something with which to appease his ravenous hunger he forgot about his missing paw and tried to use it. That must have been a very painful reminder—hence the roar.

The natives now knew that the crippled beast was still on the island. Thereafter they shut up their hogs every night— the goats had always been shut up by night. So then the lion commenced his maneating career. Even so, it would seem from what the people told me that he did not want to become a maneater and would much have preferred to live on their hogs had he been able to. He would grab a stray hog whenever he could even after he commenced killing Man.

His first human kill was an old woman who had wandered along the edge of the water close to the *matetti*, searching for driftwood for her cooking fire three evenings after the last hog had been killed. She had no time to call out; but the lion must have again hurt his injured leg because other women not far away heard him snarl loudly. But by the time they got there with some of their menfolk, the lion had dragged the body of the old woman deep into the bed of *matetti*.

On another night, during the dark period before the waning moon arose, the lion just walked into one of the huts by pushing the reed door aside and killed one of the occupants. He killed so quickly and silently that he might have removed the dead man without anyone being the wiser had he not again growled angrily, probably through again hurting himself. The deep growl awoke the victim's wife who saw the lion disappearing with her husband in his mouth. She screamed and awakened the rest of the village; but the lion was gone with his victim into the *matetti*.

This *matetti* is very difficult stuff through which to try to force your way. It grows close together and, as I have previously mentioned, the long thin leaves have points like needles. It is possible to get through it, of course, but not quickly. As you force your way through, the canes clash and rattle against one another.

After this killing the headman called his people together for a palaver. It was obvious that something would have to be done since his was about the only hut on the island strong enough to withstand the lion. He had had poles brought across from the mainland for the construction of it. The other villagers had brought no more than the absolute minimum number of poles necessary for theirs, only enough to give them a bit more stability than the *matetti* from which huts were mainly built. This meant that the lion would have no difficulty in breaking into almost any hut that took his fancy. Furthermore, the men were almost entirely unarmed except for the little axes. A very few had fish spears, which were merely a straight round piece of iron sharpened and stuck into a light shaft. They were used to pin mud-fish to the bottom in shallow water so that the owner of the spear could reach down and get hold of them. Such weapons, if you could call them that, would be little deterrent to a hungry and determined lion if he attempted to break into one of the flimsy huts.

It was the headman's suggestion that they should all collect and, with as many drums and tincans as they could raise amongst them, try to drive the lion off the island by beating him out of the *matetti*. The lower end of the island converged to a point, so if they lined up across the *matetti* and drove towards the point they might succeed. He suggested that the men go first and that the women should follow behind and to add their voices to the general hullaballu. But no woman who was carrying a small baby was to do so lest the *matetti*, springing back after someone had passed through it, should blind the infant strapped to the mother's back. The same thing might happen if anything went wrong and the mother turned to flee.

They made the attempt, but owing to the variation in the density of the *matetti* in different places, they were unable to maintain a straight line. Some forged ahead of the others. None of them could see the whole of the party. At best, each man could only see those immediately beside him.

The hunters put up the lion when about halfway through: some of them heard him growl, though nobody saw him. They redoubled their noise and were greatly encouraged when it appeared that the lion had moved on ahead of them towards the point. They continued and all seemed to be going "according to plan" until the lion reached the point and saw the river in front of him.

None of the people had ever attempted to drive a lion before. Had they commenced the drive at sundown it is probable that the lion would have taken to the water and made over towards the mainland; but he had no intention of doing so at midday. He broke back without warning and clawed down a man who had managed to get too far ahead of his companions directly on the track followed by the lion. The lion had roared savagely as he attacked the wretched man. This caused great confusion as nobody could see what was happening. In an endeavour to hear better, those close by ceased beating drums and shouting, whilst those farther away increased their noise. This no doubt had the effect of giving the lion the idea that his best escape route was straight back the way he had come. He therefore passed through the gap he had made for himself in the line of male beaters and then found only a couple of women in front of him. These two had closed in together for moral support. They turned to run but the lion was right close behind them. He sprang on one of the women and crushed her skull with a blow of his sound paw; the other he knocked flat, but she was saved by the fact that it was the lion's injured leg that hit her a glancing blow.

The man who was attacked had not had time to do more than shout, and there was so much noise going on that no one realised there was anything unusual about it. The two women, however, both screamed loudly a couple of times before the lion was on them. Their screams had been heard clearly above the general din. At once all noise stopped and people shouted to each other, asking what had happened. Those closest to the unfortunate women forced their way through the intervening *matetti* and arrived on the scene just as the second of the two women was struggling to her feet. The other was suspiciously still.

That finished the beat. The lion was now behind them, between them and the village. The hunters decided to make their way on to the point and around along the shore where the walking would be easier and where they would not meet the lion again. It was only then they found the earlier casualty. The man was badly mauled on one shoulder and right down his chest, and one ear was hanging in strips.

Although they had suffered for their excusable error in attempting to drive the lion during the midday heat, they succeeded in their purpose. For either that night or the next the lion himself left the island. Evidently he made up his mind to seek some place where he would not be confined to the extent that he had been by having only that one large belt of *matetti* in which to lie up. The islanders knew nothing of this until word came that a maneater had appeared on the mainland opposite the island. Since this was not one of those notorious maneater areas, and since they had not had a maneater around for more years than any of them could remember, they assumed it could only be the same one. They breathed a sigh of relief and hoped he would not return to plague them again.

All this I only learnt later. I had been away hunting marauding elephant in another district, and I now returned for my annual war against the buffalo. I arrived by canoe and, before making my way in to the Lagoon of Lifumba to my base-camp, pulled in at this island where there was a man here whom I supplied with onion seed each year. He grew the crop and I allowed him to keep half of it for his trouble, an arrangement which he found very profitable. My half of the crop kept me in onions for the rest of the year.

I was no sooner established in my base-camp when a deputation arrived by canoe to tell me of the maneater. I expected that, since the islanders had told me about him. There was no doubt that it was the same animal. His spoor clearly showed that he lacked one fore paw. There were many natives living along the river, from the kraal right alongside the channel that connects the lagoon with the river right away upstream to Bandari at the lower entrance to the Lupata Gorge, a distance of about six miles.

The lion prowled along this strip and had killed a number of people and also a number of their hogs. At that time he was in the vicinity of the local chief's kraal. He had made an abortive attempt there to grab a woman the previous night, but she had just managed to escape. She, like many others, was living in her lands in a shelter built about six or seven feet above the ground on stilts because the buffalo had commenced raiding the crops. She had climbed the rough ladder and was about to enter the little hut on hands and knees when she happened to glance behind her and saw the lion crouching to spring up. With great presence of mind, she scraped a large basket off the platform so that it fell down on the lion. He immediately pounced on it and thus gave the woman time to scramble into the hut, slam the reed door to, and prop it shut with a stout stick. It would have been totally inadequate protection had the hut been on the ground. The platform upon which the hut was built, however, extended only about a foot beyond the walls of the hut and the lion had no place to stand if he sprang up. Wild lion are not given to climbing ladders, and as this one lacked a front paw, he would be unable to hold on to anything and still grab.

I was asked to come and help, and I agreed at once. If you had ever lived with a maneating lion around you would realise what a ghastly condition it is, especially when living under such primitive conditions as these people were and surrounded by bush and scrub and long coarse grass still not ready for burning. If I had ever refused to respond to an S O S I could never again have looked an African in the face without shame. I had the experience and the equipment coupled with the sincere desire to help these people whom I looked upon as my friends. How could I refuse? The buffalo were bad enough, but they were nothing compared with a maneater. Anyway, I would be shooting buffalo all the time if only because we would be wanting meat for the pots. If there are buffalo around I always hunt them for that purpose.

We set off and paddled across to the lake shore, where we left the canoes and set out for the chief's kraal, about three miles away.

Chief Feira was rather a remarkable little man. Small and lightly-boned, slim and swack, with delicately-chiselled features and tiny hands and feet, one would never think he was more than half his actual age. He frankly admitted he had lost count of all the wives he had had in his life so far, though he had eleven at this time. He had not the remotest idea as to how many children they had presented him with but they were numerous. I cannot refrain from telling you of an amusing incident in this connection. On one occasion when I was in his kraal, chatting to him, I was playing with a nice little boy of about twelve years of age, a most attractive little fellow. He loved to come out with me when I was hunting buffalo and carried a cartridge bag with my pipe and tobacco and other odds and ends in it. I was very fond of him. I asked the chief whose son he was. The chief looked at him for a moment and said he did not know. Then asked the lad.

The little fellow smiled, his bright eyes twinkling and replied:

"You are, father."

The chief placed a hut at my disposal, and Saduko as usual shared it. My cook and his lad found other accommodation. About an hour after dark Feira came to our hut accompanied by another man and told me that the same woman who had previously faced the lion had heard the beast under the platform in her garden. She had called out and told this man, who was sleeping in a similar shelter not far away, that she could see the lion when she looked down through the poles that formed the floor of her shelter. He called back to tell her to keep quiet and said he would run to fetch me. It was very plucky of him because he was not far away, and there was, of course, a path running from these shelters back to the kraal, beaten out by their own feet as they went backwards and forwards between the village and the lands. And the lion would naturally use this path also. However, all was well and he arrived safely with his news.

I immediately went back with him to the lands. I need scarcely add that the chief came too: he had a most paternal attitude towards everybody in his kraal—they were probably all related to him in some way or another.

There was no sight of the lion when we got there. We could see his fresh pug marks all over the clearing in which the woman had her shelter; but at night it was not possible to find where he had left it. My shoot-lamp had a narrow concentrated beam which was not suitable for such work: it was naturally intended for more distant work. It was almost a certainty that the lion would have taken the path; but outside the clearing the path had been worn smooth before it dried. It showed no tracks of any sort. Perhaps in daylight it would be possible to see in which direction the brute had gone. So, telling the woman not to worry and that she was quite safe so long as she remained up there, and warning her not to come down until the sun was well up, we returned to the village, first taking the man back to his shelter and seeing him safely into it.

There were no alarms during the rest of the night. Next morning Saduko and I, accompanied by the chief, went out to see if we could find where the lion had gone. I was not very optimistic. The tall crops would make spooring impossible if he had gone through them, though I did not think this was very likely. Beyond the lands there was an ocean of long grass which the buffalo had not yet trampled down. It would be quite impossible to track an unwounded lion through that.

Some little distance along the path we picked up his tracks.

He was heading out towards the grass. The path stopped short at the edge of the lands: it had only been a faint track for the last hundred yards or so anyway and the lion's tracks were no longer visible. The buffalo grass stood about shoulder height, though the seed heads stood from a foot to eighteen inches higher. Shortly before we came to the edge of it I saw some white egrets fly up over it and then settle back again.

Almost certainly there were buffalo there. Egrets are a very sure indication of the presence of buffalo when they fly up like that and then settle again. They keep with the herds to feed on the innumerable insects the buff stir up out of the grass as they move through it. The birds can often be seen riding on the backs of the big black beasts. They also pick off the ticks and lice that infest their hosts and which are the reason the buffalo must have their regular mud-baths. As we could do with some meat, and as I wanted to give the chief a beast, I made over towards where I had seen the snow-white birds. There was no difficulty in the approach, apart from the difficulty in forcing a way through the grass. One did not have to worry about noise provided it was only some noise natural to the veld and not any metallic noise. The buff made plenty of noise themselves trampling down the grass and feeding.

I shot two of them before they realised what was happening. They then stampeded and quickly were lost to view in the grass. It had only been a small herd of about fifty or sixty head, so that they had not yet trampled down much of the grass. The two would be ample for the present, so I let the rest go.

We then returned to the kraal.

No word of the lion reaching us, I suggested to the chief that the woman take her children back to the kraal and I and Saduko would sleep in her shelter, taking it in turns to keep watch, since the maneater had twice on successive nights appeared there. There was just a chance that he might come again. We did so, but our vigil was fruitless.

We spent another two or three days there, but it would appear that the lion must have killed some animal, because there was no news of any human kills. I doubted very much if he would have been able to kill anything big on account of that missing paw. The only game in this stretch of country were buffalo, waterbuck, some warthog, and a few reedbuck.

I returned to my base camp, because I had left some of my boys there and I wanted to shoot a buffalo for them and see that all was well with them.

The next day I went ashore to hunt. My little lad, Friday, a born hunter if ever there was one, begged me to let him take a prowl with an old rifle I never used but with which I taught him to shoot. I had never allowed him to shoot any dangerous game, but he could go out whenever he wanted to and knock over a small buck for the pots. This pleased him enormously, boosted his confidence and also his prestige amongst his pals and all others who knew. He was also allowed to use my shotgun for duck and geese when I was busy amongst the big fellows. But I did not fancy the idea of him wandering about here with that infernal maneater somewhere around. However, Friday assured me that he would only prowl around the more open forest and scrub close to the lake shore. On the west side of Lifumba there was a fairly narrow piece of flat land covered with *mopani* forest. Practically no grass grows in Mopani forest and there are plenty of clear open spaces with small clumps of bush here and there. It is favourite country for impala, those most beautiful of little buck. I suggested he go there. There was little or no chance of him bumping the maneater in that sort of country.

I went off in the opposite direction. Having shot such buffalo as I wanted and arranged for all the meat we needed to be brought to the landing place where I had left my canoe, Saduko and I made our way back there, promising the men that I would arrange for the big canoe to be waiting for them by the time they arrived with the meat.

In due course we came to the little path which led down to the landing place and we turned along it. In places where the surface permitted I could see that someone with small feet, very small feet, had only a short time before, passed along the path in the same direction as we were going. I gradually began to feel uneasy. There did not seem to be any reason why I should; but I have long learnt not to argue with that feeling. The only possible danger there could be here would be the maneater. I had not shot and wounded any buffalo. As there was no other hunter in the district, it could only be the lion.

On my right there was a stretch of short grass which led down to the lake shore. There was a slight rise beyond it covered with light forest and scrub. To my left and immediately beside the path there was another extent of open forest but with much scrub and with four- or five-foot grass growing between the scrub and palmetto. Visibility in there was nil as far as lion were concerned. Yet that lion must be somewhere in there: he certainly was not in the short grass to my right or I could have seen him.

With my rifle at the ready, I slowly advanced. I had only taken a few paces when I saw his tracks on the path in front of me. He had come out of the scrub on my left where there happened to be a stretch of thin soft sand, almost dust, along the path. His pugs were plain, and I could easily see that he was missing the paw on his off fore. His pugs were superimposed on the footprints of whoever it was that had so recently passed along there.

It was a nasty predicament for me: Was the lion actually stalking the walker; or was it merely a coincidence that he happened to be so close behind him? I doubted the latter. Not at this hour, surely? I would have liked to hasten along in the hope that I would be in time to interfere; but perhaps I was too late anyway. The lion might already have killed, in which case he might be feeding very close to the path and would resent being disturbed. And then a sudden horrible thought occurred to me: Could it possibly be little Friday? Who else with such small feet would be walking along this path all by himself? It led nowhere but to the landing place.

I knew that Friday usually had his pal accompany him on these little hunts of his; but there were only the two of them in camp and, knowing Friday as I did, I felt pretty sure he would have told the other lad to stay there so as to be sure to have a pot of tea or coffee ready for me and Saduko whenever we got back. He often did that. It had not occurred to me to tell him not to go alone today. And yet surely he would not be here. I had heard a shot some considerable time ago and it had seemed to come from over there where I had suggested he go for the impala—it could only have been Friday.

I felt I just had to take the chance. A hunter seldom looks behind him, and I knew that Africans do not worry about danger that is not apparent. I also knew that they rarely have this inner intuition that warns of imminent danger. No matter who it was I simply had to push along and hope to be in time. I knew I would never forgive myself if it was Friday and if I had allowed him to be killed because I was being too cautious. In spite of the strong sense of danger close to me, and fresh pug marks of the maneater on the path in front, I hastened forward.

I was very fond of Friday, one of the finest little fellows I have ever met. I did not run because I might have need of a quick shot and I did not want to become winded; but I walked just as quickly as I could. Like all native footpaths, this one twisted a bit to avoid obstacles and I could never see more than about twenty-five to thirty yards ahead. Then I turned a corner around a bush and came into view of the lake. There was a clear stretch here of about fifty yards. Friday was about halfway across it and he was staggering under the weight of a young impala which he was carrying across his shoulders and between the legs of which he had tied his rifle. Between us was the maneater. The brute was trying to hurry to get a bit closer before making his rush. The lion must have realised that his missing paw was a great handicap (he had without doubt missed many a seemingly easy kill because of it). He had to limp badly as the injured leg was still much too sore to be used.

It was a difficult situation for me. Friday was in the direct line of fire and I could only put a bullet into the lion's hind-quarters. That would surely cripple him; but things can sometimes go wrong, and I had been hurrying. I might slightly misplace my bullet. It wasn't good enough.

I dropped to one knee so as to get a level shot and shouted. That did it. The lion spun around to stand broadside-on and look back the way he had come: Friday also stopped and looked back. My rifle spoke and the maneater dropped with a soft-nose bullet slap through his shoulder. He never budged again. Friday's face was a picture!

I mentioned the two previous escapes of Friday. This was the third very narrow escape he had from a maneating lion.

It seems that he had shot an impala out of a troop of them but his bullet had gone clean through and wounded a young one standing immediately beyond. The first one had been killed outright, but this other had run. It was clear that the impala had been hard hit or he would not have left the remainder of the troop. Friday had of course followed. It had been a fairly long chase and the little buck was dead when the lad found him. Then, as he was closer to the landing place than to where he had left his canoe, Friday had brought the little buck here. He had intended to leave it and then return to collect the first kill and his canoe. He had forgotten all about the lion and had not the foggiest notion that the brute had been following him and was just about to rush him!

I back-spoored the maneater to see just what had happened. As well as I could reconstruct it he must have been lying-up about ten yards from the path. Then his nostrils had been assailed by a curious mixture of scents: man, buck, and fresh blood. The breeze had been blowing across from the path to where he was lying. He must have joined the path very soon after Friday had passed but not before the boy had turned one of the many corners around a bush. Maneaters will always try to ambush their quarry if they possibly can, and it could be that this one was hoping that Friday would halt for a few moments and so give him a chance to slip up past him and lie in wait. But, fortunately for him, Friday did not stop. He knew he was close to the landing place and even if he had wanted to stop for any reason he would have waited so as not to have to put down and pick up his load, which was a heavy one for so young a lad.

The Maccuan Maneaters

ALONG the Portuguese East African coast—and, for that matter, along the coasts of Tanganyika and Kenya—there is a belt of dense impenetrable thorn-bush. There are gaps here and there, but generally speaking this belt extends right the whole way along. In some places it is wider than in others. It is to be found from north of the Zambezi mouths to away north of Lamu. Throughout there is a fairly dense native population which has made clearings in the bush at the cost of immense labour. If they slacken their efforts in the slightest the bush will overgrow the clearing in a remarkably short space of time.

In this type of country there is little game to be found as there is little or no grass. A few bushbuck are there and too many bush pig; but not much else. Leopard, of course, and occasionally in some parts a few buffalo appear from time to time. But these latter are not residents.

But there are lion here—only they know why. The bush pig, of course, would be an attraction (lion are very fond of pig); but lion would get very much easier hunting if they were to move out of the coastal belt, sometimes only a few miles, to more open country where there is plenty of game of all kinds. Instead of doing so they take to maneating. Throughout this entire coastal belt you will find maneaters. Some stretches are worse than others; but it can safely be stated without fear of contradiction that no stretch is ever entirely free from the scourge for more than a short period. It may be a few months, it may be a few years, but sooner or later the drums will roll out their warning through the night.

The Maccua stretch, which runs along the hinterland of Mozambique, is one of the very worst stretches of the lot. This was one of the bad areas referred to by Livingstone. I have hunted maneaters there on three different occasions and can say that this area is just as bad today as it was in Livingstone's day. The maneaters romp the countryside in bands of three, four and five. As elsewhere, you occasionally find two and even more rarely a solitary lion; but three seems to be the favourite number.

It is utterly impossible to spoor them, for the thorn is un-believably dense. It would be extremely difficult for a man to get through it even if he lay flat down and edged along by means of his elbows and toes—hands and knees would be quite out of the question. But since the ground in there is covered with a fine compost consisting of myriads of the tiny leaves that drop off the bush annually (no fires ever reach in here), no tracks much less pug marks can be seen. Lion that live under these conditions have no mane: if they had it would soon be pulled out. So that you do not even get an occasional long hair to help you follow them.

Then again, even supposing you had managed to keep on their tracks, what good is it going to do you? They will be lying down and motionless: you will be moving. They will inevit-ably spot you first and move off. Even if they do not, how are you going to get your rifle into action? If you succeed in getting it to your shoulder you have not one chance in a hundred thousand of placing your shot accurately. The bullet will inevitably be deflected before it reaches its target.

It is the merest waste of time and energy—as I well know. The first time I went down there to hunt a party of three of the brutes which had been playing havoc for some months, I tried all the accepted methods of hunting maneaters, including spooring them into this impossible bush. My efforts were without avail. I had not had as much experience then with man-eaters as I have now; but I learned a lot during the many weeks I was there which has proved of great help since.

On that first occasion I had no motor transport, so when word came in of a kill somewhere I, not knowing any better, would pack up and trek off whether it was half-a-dozen miles away or a dozen or more. I was very keen and wanted the local natives to see that I was willing to do anything I could to help them. All I was really doing, however, was to tire myself and my porters needlessly.

On arrival, if there was sufficient light left I would endeavour to pick up the spoor and track the maneaters. Failing in that I would ask for a goat to be tied up and would sit up over it all night in the hope of getting a shot. I had yet to learn that the maneaters would be miles away and laughing at me; I had yet to learn that maneaters in these sort of places in Africa practically never return to a kill. And that, of course, is one of the things that makes the hunting of them so difficult. Having fed they wander away and may or may not kill again for a couple of days. They keep on the go, and the result is that the next kill will usually be many miles away. And there was I trekking off after them once more to go through the same performance yet again. It took me about three weeks to realise that the lion could play this game with me indefinitely if I did not think up some better method.

I put on my thinking cap and after much deep thought came up with two alternatives which seemed worth trying. I decided to try first the one that had first occurred to me (because I didn't at all like the second one!). It seemed to me that the only thing to do was to try to outguess the brutes and get to some kraal *before* they attacked. Experience had shown that it was no earthly use getting there afterwards. A good map of the district showing all the kraals would have been a great help, but

I was quite sure that no such map existed. Well then, I would have to make my own. So I called up the local chief and his various headmen and told them what I wanted. They proved very helpful, and whenever they were in doubt they were able to produce someone who could give me the desired information. So on a large sheet of brown paper, the only large piece of paper I possessed, I drew a map.

It took quite a while because Africans know nothing about miles or kilometres and speak of distances by pointing to the position the sun will be in when they get there—assuming a start at sunrise and, of course, walking. And it is necessary to allow for *their* walking when without loads, not yours. So to avoid too many alterations on my map I had them draw their notions on the sandy ground with a stick, and then after there had been the usual discussion and argument about the exact location of some outlying kraal, I would copy that particular section on to my paper.

After half a day, which they thoroughly enjoyed, I had what I hoped was an accurate map of the district showing each and every kraal, large and small, and the many small paths through the thorn leading from one to another. This would enable me to cut across at times instead of making wide and needlessly long treks on better-worn paths. Of course, in many instances there were no short-cuts from some of the kraals to others: the bush in between had been much too impenetrable for the people even to attempt to beat a track through it.

Now I had to try to plot the maneaters' route by marking on my map the kraals where kills had taken place. This was to prove more difficult than the making of the map, because the information would be valueless unless I got the kills in their correct sequence. Naturally, they couldn't be expected to remember the sequence of all the many kills that had taken place during the months the lion had been ravaging the district; so I had them start with the most recent and work back from there. There was no doubt about the last three or four; it was when they tried to get back beyond that that the arguments started. When kills take place in some of the remoter parts, unless the African has a relative there or a particular friend, he takes little notice—if a thing is remote from him he is little interested in it. But I kept them at it for the rest of the day until I felt there was nothing left that they could tell me. After they had left I sat down to study my map and plan a campaign.

It was immediately obvious that it was not going to be easy. The lion did not hold to any very definite route, though there seemed to be a tendency for them to work around in an anti-clockwise direction. There were considerable variations in the distances between kills which were not explained by the different distances between kraals, although that naturally had a bearing on it. However, the extent of the kill was probably the answer. When they happened to kill and carry away more than one person they would be better fed and therefore one might expect them to travel farther before killing again.

It would be mainly guess-work, but my map would enable me to reduce my guesses to something like a system. But there was a point which I had not allowed for and which also probably had a bearing on the irregularity of the kills. That was that in some of the kraals the people kept up their precautions so that even if the maneaters had visited them they were unable to secure a kill and were compelled to move on to some other kraal where perhaps they found some man or woman who had foolishly relaxed those precautions. It is an astonishing thing how soon some Africans, especially the older ones, will take the most fantastic risks even when they know very well there are maneaters about. Yet they will always shout to the children, whether their own or someone else's, warning them that the sun is dropping and telling them to go into the huts and stay there. So it is not that they have forgotten about the danger. They themselves, however, will sit there talking until dark; will go out to the bush to relieve themselves then or during the night; or will do so at crack of dawn—one of the worst possible times if there is a maneater around. The lion seem to know perfectly well that by dawn someone will be wanting to come out and empty his bladder. Lion will spend hours, sometimes the entire night, in a village obviously just waiting for dawn and the certainty of someone emerging from a hut. I have seen where it has happened many times.

My first attempt to out-guess the maneaters was a failure: they killed at a kraal several miles short of where I had gone. I heard the drums in the distance but knew from bitter experience that it was no use going there—I would be much too late. My second attempt was also a flop; this time the lion by-passed the kraal where I was awaiting them; and again to my chagrin I heard the drums beating. I had known there would be disappointments. It would have been too much to hope that I would out-guess them every time, especially after they had been working the district for months; but it was very upsetting to think of those unfortunate people being killed owing to my ineptitude. So I made up my mind to try the alternative method I had considered. This was to have a lion-trap built on the road that ran past the chief's kraal. The natives everywhere know how to build these traps; but usually they only build them for leopard which have been killing their goats. If built for lion they are much more massive, but the principle is the same.

The trap is an oblong structure built of stout poles well-sunk in the ground and firmly lashed together. The top consists of similar poles with as many and as large rocks as they can find and lift piled on top. There are generally two compartments the smaller of which may contain a live goat as bait or possibly some meat that is a bit high—though Africans would prefer to eat the meat rather than use it as bait! The trap is just wide enough to accommodate a lion or leopard, as the case may be, so that he cannot turn around. There is a stout trap-door which drops down into place behind the lion when he enters and shoves his nose into the trip or, depending on the design, stands on the trip. The natives come around next morning and kill the beast by jabbing spears in between the poles.

It was my intention to sit in the goat compartment, offering myself as bait. I doubted if a goat would interest the maneaters sufficiently; and anyway the moon was nearly full so that I knew that my carbide shooting lamp (I had not yet an electric one) would be useless. If a lion trapped himself we would certainly get him. I hoped, however, to bag more than one if I was so close to them as all that. I might add that the natives here had tried to trap maneaters before, using goats as bait; but they had only killed an occasional one. They had never tried to use one of themselves as bait and, since they had no fire-arms of any sort, one can scarcely blame them. They were flabbergasted when I told them that I intended to sit in the goat compartment. But when I pointed out that my lamp was useless when there was a good moon, and that nothing must be done to stop the killing, they somewhat reluctantly agreed to build the trap. They finished it that day and, since my guess-work had indicated that the maneaters were due to visit the chief's kraal tonight or tomorrow, I took up my position in it and had my men shut me securely into the goat side. They then returned to the hut the chief had placed at our disposal.

They had only been gone about half an hour when the man-eaters arrived. They came from behind me, because I had been sitting facing into the trap. The first intimation I had of their presence was when I heard a deep sigh right beside me. I glanced around and there, sure enough, was an almost maneless lion standing looking in at me. He was not more than eighteen inches away. Beyond him was a lioness. I am sure I could have killed him; but I had had my rifle with the muzzles sticking just through into the main part of the trap. I would have had to withdraw it and then turn it around and shove the muzzles through the side of my compartment. The lion might or might not have waited. What I wanted was for one of the brutes to enter the trap before I opened fire, so that I could be sure of him anyway—because they certainly would not enter it after I commenced shooting. I had figured that I might be able to shoot at least one if not both of the others before bothering about the one in the trap. But this was such a fantastically easy shot that I was on the point of withdrawing my rifle from the trap when the third beast, another lioness, settled the matter. She had come around the other side of the trap and, seeing the open entrance, evidently thought she had only to make a rush and she would have me. She made her rush and came up with a bump against the poles forming the division between the two compartments. At the same time the trapdoor dropped behind her. She growled angrily when she found the bars between us and savagely clawed at them. It was on the offchance that there might be a weakness in the construction that I had had the muzzles of my rifle protruding into the main section of the trap, as I had no hankering to have a lion's paw come through and claw me.

When I saw that there was no immediate danger of that happening, I glanced around and saw that the other lioness had moved around and was now standing outside the trapdoor. The lion was still on my right watching to see what his mate was doing in the trap. None of them yet knew that she couldn't get out—she hadn't yet tried to: she was still endeavouring to get at me. I brought my rifle around, shoved the muzzles through the side of the trap, and killed the lion instantly where he stood. On the heels of the shot the lioness in the trap loosed a shattering roar and tried to jump back, only to come up against the trapdoor. Since she was looking towards me with her mouth not more than about two and a half feet from my ear, she nearly deafened me. She now tried to spring on me. She gave vent to another terrific roar as she launched herself at the bars between us; but fortunately she was too close to them to be able to gain any momentum. I brought the rifle around and, as she scrabbled and clawed furiously at the poles, I shot her in the chest from a range of about a foot. She subsided with a deep groan. The second lioness, the only survivor now, was still somewhere outside beyond the door; but I could not see her at first. Then after a few moments I saw her making off into the bush. She stopped on the edge of the thorn; but I was unable to bring the rifle to bear on account of the number of poles forming the trap. I shouted to my men that all was well and that they could come and let me out.

The entire village came with them. There was great excitement. They had all heard the trapdoor fall and were wondering what was happening when they did not immediately hear a shot. They had naturally thought that I would shoot as soon as anything entered the trap. Then, when they heard the trapped lioness's furious roars after my first shot, they imagined I had only wounded her. When they heard her deep groan after the second shot they knew she was dead. Their delight was unbounded when they came around the trap and saw the dead lion also.

But I had to warn them that there was still one lioness around, and that she was almost certain to stick around close all night and possibly the next day, wondering what had happened to her mate and companion. I felt so sure that she would come back and look for them, that I told my fellows I would sit-up for her. Since my using myself as bait had proved so successful, nobody tried to dissuade me.

H

And this is where I made a mistake—lack of experience being my excuse. Without thinking I allowed my men to shut me into the goat compartment again, leaving the two dead man-eaters where they lay.

For a couple of hours nothing happened. Then I saw a shadow that could only be the lioness slinking along in the deeper shadow of the thorn thrown by the moon. I made no move. I wanted a much better shot than that in order to make sure. But she would not give me a better shot. She must know that I was still there in the trap and must realise that her companions were dead. Presumably she associated me with their death, and not unreasonably. Had I sat somewhere else she might have approached the trap; but there was nowhere else in the vicinity where I could have sat and gotten a shot: there was no tree worthy of the name, no hut with a doorway facing directly on to the trap. Because of the moon it would have been no use my sitting in some other hut and attempting to approach on foot. The lioness would have seen me coming long before I was within night range as there was no cover near the trap except the continuous thorn-bush beyond it. When shooting lion at night without any cover at all, it is essential to have a light that will show up one's sights and also one's target. A lion is not going to attack something it cannot see, therefore one's shooting lamp must be capable of dazzling the animal. The old carbide lamps were not able to do that if there was much moonlight. Even the modern electric ones are not much use in moonlight.

The lioness roamed around and around keeping ever in the shadow and never keeping still. On account of the poles I could not keep my rifle swinging to cover her long enough to get a shot. I tried again and again, but it was no use. I did not want to wound her. She was quite bad enough as she was. From time to time she would disappear in the bush and I thought she had gone; but after a while I would see her again. And so it went on all night.

Finally, when the eastern sky was greying she disappeared for the last time. Not once had she given me even a fair chance of a shot.

I was tired after my all-night vigil as I had had no sleep the previous day in the anxiety to make sure that the trap was built to my liking. Ordinarily, I would have been quite happy to leave it to the locals, but not when I was going to be the bait myself! So, after breakfast, I turned in. I was very disappointed at not bagging that second lioness; but needless to say the locals brushed that aside as not worth consideration. Had I not slain two of the brutes?

The lioness had been dragged out of the trap and skinned, as also had the lion. I had the two carcases left close in front of the trap and this night I sat in the trap itself with the door removed. If the lioness came back tonight surely I'd get a shot at her. But much to my disappointment there was no sign of her.

For several days there was no word of her. She must have killed a bushpig or something and be living on that. And then she returned.

In spite of my repeated warnings, one woman was foolish. True, when there was no news of the lion for so long most of the villagers, like the rest of the population of the district, believed that the lioness had cleared out of the district, perhaps to search for another mate, and to a very great extent, relaxed their precautions. But this particular woman was particularly careless. She had gone with a party of women and children to the water. This was quite usual when the water was some distance away from the kraal, whether there are maneaters about or not; but the women generally all return together— most certainly they do if there are maneaters around. The maneaters' favourite method is to grab a woman coming back from the water in the evening all by herself. And that is what happened now. Her companions had started back telling her she ought to hurry that they had waited long enough. But she dawdled over her toilet until the other women were out of sight. She then started back with her pot of water on her head, herding her little daughter in front of her along the path. The other women, who were about a hundred and fifty yards or more along the path and around a slight bend in it, heard a shrill scream followed by a series of screams of terror obviously being made by a child. They put down their pots of water and ran back to the bend in the path. Here they met the little girl running towards them and still screaming. One of the women clutched the little child and tried to comfort her, while the others looked around the bend. There they saw the missing lioness crouching beside the body of the little girl's mother.

Leaving their water pots, some of the younger ones raced along the path to the village ulululuing at the top of their voices in a way that carries a great distance. I heard the voices and guessed the cause. Grabbing up my rifle, I started down the path towards them. I did not wait to be told anything. They came back with me as far as the bend, telling me all I needed to know on the way. I stopped them here and continued on my own. Fortunately, there was none of that infernal thorn just here. The lioness had sneaked across the more or less open patch to a clump of grass and lain in ambush there. She had allowed the party of women to pass and awaited that inevitable straggler. But it was the last straggler she was ever to grab. She offered me an easy shot and I took the fullest advantage of it.

The Daki Man-Killing Marauder

WHEN in the Chikoa district, south of the Zambezi, word reached me of a bad elephant. Not only was he an inveterate crop-raider and breaker-open of granaries, but he was also a killer.

In this area the lands are often some considerable distance from the village, and it is quite customary for the people to build granaries out there in the lands. As the crop is harvested it is placed in these granaries. Later it may or may not be removed and brought in to the kraal. In the kraal the granaries are sometimes built inside the living huts, and sometimes immediately outside them. Those outside and those in the lands have a conical thatched roof like a hat which can easily be pushed on one side so that the owner can get at the stored grain.

It is by no means unusual for some old elephant bull to discover that he can get an easy feed from these granaries. This type of raider is usually solitary though occasionally there are a pair of them. I cannot remember ever finding cows raiding granaries. In the kraal these granaries will mostly be built on low platforms perhaps eighteen inches to two feet off the ground; but out in the lands they may be anything up to six feet above the ground.

It occasionally happens that some old bull develops a taste for alcohol. They will then get very drunk by guzzling over-ripe wild fruit which will ferment in their vast stomachs; but when the wild-fruit season is past they still have their hankering for drink. It is then that they become the most determined raiders of granaries, returning night after night in order to replenish their vats, because the grain will also ferment.

The elephant seem to know how much water to add to the brew to obtain the desired effect.

Elephant can and do get fighting drunk, and can be very dangerous when "under the influence". This may sound absurd to the general reader; but any truly experienced elephant-hunter will corroborate. What is more, they can and do suffer from hang-overs and, like their human counterparts, are then apt to be bad-tempered and liverish. And it is when they are either drunk or more probably suffering from the after effects that they are so determined to get at the stored grain. No amount of noise that the wretched owners can create will have any effect: it is only when a very brave man approaches with a blazing grass torch that the raider can sometimes be persuaded to move on and raid somewhere else.

It sometimes happens that the elephant turns on that man and kills him. It is also not unknown for the raider to get annoyed at the noise being made by the occupants of the hut when he smashes a hole in the roof and reaches in with his trunk searching for the interior granary. He will sometimes just lean against the hut, thereby smashing it down on top of its unfortunate occupants. He is quite likely then to trample on them as they are trapped under the roof, in his continued search for the grain he is determined to have. Naturally, such a midnight visitor has a most demoralising effect on the village. He is so huge and so rough and the unarmed human being is so utterly helpless against him.

One elephant had almost completely wiped out a fair-sized village overnight. It happened that there was a strong wind blowing and when he smashed down the hut he was raiding the fallen roof took fire, and as the huts were built rather close together, sparks flew and set fire to the thatch of other roofs which in turn fired others. The occupants of the first hut were burned to death.

I arrived at the local chief's village, which was roughly in the centre of the area that was being disturbed by the raider. The chief told me that the brute was much worse now than he had been. Some pseudo hunter who had been passing through had shot at and wounded him but had not bothered to follow him up and finish him. The hunter's excuse was that he was in a hurry, but the chief and the local natives knew that the real reason was that the man did not like walking and was much too scared to follow any wounded and potentially dangerous beast, much less one with so bad a reputation as this bull. Once again the deaths of several innocent natives could be chalked up against a nervous and inexperienced "sportsman": a man who thought nothing of wounding an animal and then going his way uncaring; but a man who would certainly like all his friends and acquaintances to class him as a big-game hunter. I have met all too many of them.

The direct result of his wounding this bull was to turn him into a definite man-killing rogue. The elephant liked to wait close to some path much frequented by natives and then, when the unsuspecting travellers passed by, he would charge out without warning, chase them and kill any he could catch. And all too often he would succeed. Of course, when word got around the district anyone passing that way would give the favoured spot a wide berth; but the killer soon realised that and found another equally good place on another path. As he was not expected there he played havoc for several days until his presence became known. But there were other paths and there were always natives going somewhere, and nobody knew where he was likely to be. He must be killed.

But I realised he would not be easy to contact. By all accounts he got around the district from end to end and from centre to extremities. There was no telling where he was going to appear next. He lived in this area and had been known for several years. At first he had merely raided the crops and was not dangerous. But he had gradually commenced to raid the granaries also when the crops had been harvested. It was then that he started to become a nuisance, but only during the past twelve months or so had he become a killer. Even at that his exploits had been comparatively trivial beside what he had become since he had been wounded some three months ago. His wound must have been painful without being fatal or incapacitating.

When I arrived there it was the most difficult time of the year in which to hunt. The rains were over and the grass was at its longest and strongest with those infernal grass-seeds all ready to fall and stick into one, but the grass not yet dry enough to burn. There was certainly no pleasure in hunting at that season—it was just sheer hard labour and most exasperating. To make it even more difficult there were various other herds of elephant in the district and several lone bulls and pairs and trios of bulls besides the rogue. It was a fine district for elephant as I well knew: I had hunted here on different occasions in the past. But on those occasions I had not been hunting any one particular beast which made it very much easier. With so much spoor about and so much of the long coarse grass trampled down it was going to be a matter of fine tracking to hunt down the rogue. I could anticipate many abortive hunts when we would lose his spoor through having it over-run by the tracks of some of the other elephant.

As soon as word got around the district that I was there to hunt the rogue, news began to come in. I was listening to a report of the rogue—at least the report of a lone bull—having raided some crops a few miles away when another man arrived with an account of a lone bull having raided his crops.

Since the two men had come from different directions, each about the same distance away, was it two different raiders or was it the same one? That was a question which could only be answered by following the spoor and seeing if it led from one lot of lands to the other lot; about five or six miles away in a more or less direct line. But the difficulty was to know which crops had been raided first. And here neither of the men could help because neither of them had heard the raider and only knew of the raid when they went around their lands after sun-up.

I decided to go out to the first man's lands simply because he had been the first arrival. The other chap came along with us, hoping that I would go to his lands if I was unable to come up with this raider.

We were able to follow the spoor for about three or four miles, then lost it hopelessly when the tracks of a herd of about thirty elephant crossed it. We searched and searched but could not find it again. The bull might have turned along the same route followed by the herd so that their tracks wiped his out completely. The dry ground and the trampled down grass made it quite impossible to identify any one individual track from another of approximately the same size.

We admitted defeat and returned to the place where we had started. I had managed to get by car to the kraal where the owner of the raided crops lived. My gunbearer and I, accompanied by the owner of the second raided garden, drove off there as he told me I could get quite close by car. What a saving in time and energy a car can be! Of course one can never hunt elephant by car; but nowadays there are dry-season roads through most districts which helps enormously. A day's trek on foot with porters can be covered in an hour by car; whilst a day's run by car would take a week or ten days on foot.

As we had to pass my camp at the chief's kraal we halted there for a pot of tea; then on to the raided lands. Here we went through much the same performance as at the other place except that we did not follow the spoor of the raider so far before it also disappeared under the spoor of almost certainly the same herd that had wiped out the other lot. So it was impossible to say whether or not it had been the same animal that raided both crops.

But the following day definite word came in of the rogue. Somewhere about the middle of the forenoon, a breathless runner, dripping with perspiration, arrived and gasped out that the rogue was only three miles away and had killed an old man. As soon as the runner had had a drink of water, I bundled him into the utility and we drove off as fast as the road would permit and as far along it as possible. During the drive, the man told me that he and three others had been coming along a path when there was a sudden screaming trumpet-blast from the bush right beside them. They had dropped their loads and run for their lives. But the last man in the file had been an old fellow and the rogue had had no difficulty in catching him. He had only had time to cry out once. Knowing that they could do nothing to help him and that he must have been killed almost instantly, the three survivors continued to run until they reached the nearest kraal. They had then been told about me, so this chap had run in to get me.

The kraal they had reached was as far as we could go by car. All three said they would come with me as they wanted to collect their possessions. I had no objection.

We only had about a mile and a half to go. And just as I saw the bundles lying on the ground where they had been dropped, I suddenly felt that familiar inner warning of danger, danger very near. The rogue was still here. I halted and in a whisper warned the men to keep close to me, otherwise I would be unable to help them if the rogue realised our presence and attacked. The breeze was fitful. I had, of course, noticed that as soon as we started walking. The elephant-hunter must always know how the breeze is moving no matter how light it is.

I moved very slowly forward until I came to a small gap in the bush. As the rogue had his ambush in this bush I commenced to edge quietly into this gap in the hope of seeing him before he knew we were there. He would probably be facing the path waiting for another victim to come along it, so that I might be lucky enough to get an easy broadside shot at him. Had it been an ordinary bull I was hunting I would have worried about the fitfulness of the breeze, because if the elephant got a whiff of man he would go for his life. But this was a rogue killer. So far, if he scented man near him he attacked. But since he was so close I would prefer to get my shot at him before he came for me. If an African elephant is almost on top of you it is by no means easy to drop him instantly: it depends greatly just how he is carrying his trunk. I knew I could prevent myself from being trampled or grabbed; but I was not alone—I had also to think of the men who were with me. It would have been wiser to have left them at the kraal and told them to stay there until they heard a shot. However, it was too late to think about that now.

And then I felt a cool draught on the back of my neck. That meant that the rogue would get it. I quickly stepped forward to see around the bush as I expected an instantaneous charge. But to my astonishment, I was barely in time to see the bush closing in behind him like a curtain as he disappeared beyond it! There was no time for a shot although I had, of course, had my rifle ready for instant use. He was gone. Deadly and all as he was where unarmed natives were concerned, the whiff of a white man so close to him put him to flight.

We then searched for the remains of the old man. It was a pitiful sight. It would seem that the rogue had grabbed him with his trunk and then slammed him savagely against a tree, which must have killed him instantly. Not satisfied with that, however, he had then placed a mighty forefoot on the body and literally pulled it to pieces, flinging arms and legs and head far and wide. The trunk he had trampled almost out of recognition. And as though that wasn't enough, he had been awaiting another passer-by. If only that little draught hadn't come from the wrong direction just too soon!

My gunbearer and I followed for hours but were unable to come up with him. He had evidently had a very bad scare and was making himself scarce. The elephant had merely to hasten away to wherever he wanted to go, but we had to spoor him laboriously. It was easy enough at first because he had been running and then dropped to that deceptively fast shuffling stride that elephant use when frightened and just over their first panic. The length of stride they take is extraordinary and they can sweep along at about eight miles an hour and keep it up for hours on end, although if you happened to see them passing broadside-on to you, you would think they were scarcely doing half that speed. It was after he dropped into this fast long-distance gait that the following of him became so much more difficult. As we were heading away from camp and as there was no indication that he was slowing down, I finally turned back. I have never before seen an elephant so determined to change his locality. He had made a bee-line for somewhere, and it must have been somewhere distant. There was no slowing down; no stopping for a rest or to look back. He would have been miles ahead of us even if we had been able to walk fast, and we had not been able to do that on account of the difficulty we had in making sure we were really on his spoor.

It was a great disappointment after getting so close to him. But nobody was to blame. No matter how great his experience no hunter has yet learned how to control the wind. The long trudge back to camp after such a disappointment is heartbreaking. This was not the first time I had had a man-killing rogue flee when he got a whiff of my wind. I had hunted another some years previously which had acted very much as this one had: ambushing and killing harmless natives after someone had wounded and left him. The elephant had absolutely no fear of natives; but obviously had of white men—at any rate of white men who were not scared of him. I had long learnt that animals, especially elephant, know perfectly well if the hunter is frightened of them, and, if not, are not nearly so likely to attack. On the contrary, as in this case, they are much more inclined to beat it for safer parts. Had this one attacked I would have had him.

As I did not expect to hear of the rogue for at least a week after the way he had fled, I shot several good elephant that had been raiding crops and also some meat for my own pot. I did not want to do any shooting if I had reason to believe that the rogue was near in case I scared him off again. I also succeeded in tracking down two lone bulls—quite possibly the two I had first hunted. So if a lone bull now turned up raiding it would probably be the rogue.

And then again we got news of the killer. It appeared that two young fellows had gone wandering along the Daki river, which only ran during the rains though water could usually be got by digging, searching for wild honey. They were unexpectedly attacked by a big bull elephant which could only have been the rogue. Thanks to the nature of the bush just there and the fact that they were not on a path—there was none—the rogue had not been ambushing them and so was not as close as he would have liked to have been. Their agility and fleetness of foot saved them. Evidently, he was just lying low, away out there far from habitation. It was quite apparent that he was still deadly and fully prepared to kill if he thought he could get away with it.

I went out with ten days' tucker and camped out there on the Daki in the vicinity of where the two young men had been attacked. They came with me as guides. But although we hunted around extensively, the rogue had moved away and we failed to find him. After a week of it I quit. There was nothing to be gained by staying there any longer, and I might be missing chances elsewhere.

We then had several calls to spoor up a long bull which had been raiding the crops in various widely-separated parts of the district. If these were the rogue's spoor, he was certainly playing safe. On each occasion we had so far to go that we were unable to come up with him. After all, he could keep on wandering right through the night whereas we could only spoor him while there was sufficient light to see the tracks. I felt confident that it was the rogue. No ordinary bull, with nothing more on his conscience than a raid on the crops would feel any need to make himself so scarce after each raid. There was nobody here except myself following-up marauders, and I was not doing anything like so much of it as I would have liked to do in case I drove the man-killer away—and I was determined to slay him.

I had two more abortive chases after him during the following weeks. On the first, the wind again let me down at the last moment although I was not as close to him as I had been the time he killed the old man. All the same, if the wind had not suddenly changed I would probably have killed him that time. On the second occasion we again lost his spoor through having it wiped out by other elephant.

At last the gods relented. I was called out to deal with a

lone bull that was actually then raiding a crop only a short mile away. As it was about 10 o'clock in the morning, that was very unusual. I lost no time getting there. The owner of the crop pointed up to my left where there was a slight rise in the ground and whispered that the raider was up there. A finger, as it were, of the garden ran up there over the little rise. There was forest and much bush all around the finger, but there was no sign of a raiding elephant. The millet was not so tall as elsewhere, standing only about nine feet high, and that was not high enough to conceal an African elephant. A good deal of the crop had been trampled down by previous raiders, including quite a stretch of it between where I was standing and about halfway up along that finger. And then I saw the raider.

He was standing behind a clump of bush right on the edge of the garden up on the righthand side of the finger. The bush was big enough to completely conceal him. But now he just swayed forward moving only one forefoot and reached out into the millet with his trunk. He swept a generous trunk-full of the grain into his possession and then taking it with him, swayed back again behind his bush where he ate it without the slightest chance of being seen. I waited to see how long he would be before again showing himself. Since we were standing quite motionlessly he would not know us from three tree stumps. After he had again swept a trunk full of millet away and drawn back behind his bush, I promptly moved as quickly and as quietly towards him as possible, but stopped shortly before he was due to reappear. We were right out in the open: there was no cover of any sort. Yet he never noticed us. He was entirely unsuspicious of danger. But I wanted to get still closer because he kept his great shoulder behind the bush, so that I would have to take a brain-shot. There is no rerl diffi-culty in a side brain-shot but the bullet must be accurately placed and I would, of course, be firing from the standing off-hand position. I like to be certain. So we stood like three features of the landscape while he was in view, and then, when he once more withdrew, we advanced and halted within about fifteen strides of the bush that hid him. The breeze was steady and favourable. We waited. Once more and for the last time he swayed forward into view. My heavy bullet crashed into his brain and he never knew that a rifle had been fired. It was as easy as that. Yet it had taken me six weeks to get that shot.

At first we could not be sure that this really was the rogue. I felt confident it was because I had already shot all the lone bulls known to be in the district. But another might have come from somewhere. However, I was so sure that it was the bad one, that I did not hesitate to get out after other raiders now. They also had to be taught their lesson.

Some idea of the elephant's intelligence can be gained by reviewing the rogue's method of raiding in broad daylight. That in itself was very unusual; but so was the cunning he displayed in exposing himself as little as possible and for as short a time as possible. And I am sure he was so cautious simply because of my presence in the district. He had shown himself to be so contemptuous of the natives, that I can scarcely imagine he would have cared whether they saw him or not during his raid.

Naturally, I could not leave the district until I was quite certain it was freed of its scourge. There were plenty of elephant to keep me busy, so that did not matter. When no news of a killer came in during the next six weeks, and I seemed to have succeeded in discouraging the raiding—and since anyway most of the crops had been harvested by then—I moved on with the gratitude of the entire district for the help I had given to them.

I wonder why so many writers on Africa speak slightingly of

the native and almost without exception state that he has no sense of gratitude. Could it be that those writers had never attempted to do anything for the African that might have aroused his sense of gratitude? I have been hunting and living continuously amongst the Africans for some thirty-five years now and I have never found any lack of gratitude when gratitude might be expected. It must be remembered that the African has no word for "thanks" in any of his languages. He therefore shows his gratitude not in words like the white man, but in deeds—possibly long afterwards.

The Mandimba Maneaters

O F all the notorious area for maneaters known to me I
sometimes think that the one about which I now speak
is the worst. It also was one of those mentioned by
David Livingstone. It runs from Mandimba on the Portuguese
side of the border up along the river to Mangochi on the
British side with the third point of the triangle near Namwera.
This is a thickly populated area with the result that there is not
much game about. But there are all too many bush-pig and
warthog—two of the lion's favourite dishes,

When I think of each of these bad districts and start to tell of
them I get the same feeling about each of them in turn. There is
the notorious coastal belt; there is another bad stretch in
southern Nyasaland; the one along the lower Zambezi valley
in P.E.A.; another up on Lake Nyasa; this one I am about to
tell you of along the Portuguese border; then almost the entire
Lindi province in Tanganyika is infested with the brutes; and
there is the notorious Usori district—notorious for its "lion-
men" as well as for its maneaters—also in Tanganyika; whilst
the Nyika thorn desert in which Paterson shot his famous
Tsavo maneaters still has a deservedly bad name for maneaters.

The white population in Africa, as well as throughout the
rest of the world, knows little or nothing about these scourges
because the victims are all natives and few people care much
about them. Most certainly the newspapers do not consider
them worth space. It is a very different thing if a white man
happens to be carried off; but that has not occurred for many
years. The well-known Tsavo maneaters would probably never

have been heard of if they had not been responsible for a three or six weeks (I forget which) stoppage of the construction of the railroad from Mombasa to Lake Victoria; the coolie labourers who had been imported from India struck and refused to work until the maneaters had been shot out. These lion had the doubtful honour of being mentioned in Parliament. Moreover, these lion killed at least two white men and ate one of them. There was also mention made in the Press of a maneater in the Chikwawa district many years ago who carried off a bank clerk who had gone down there to hunt with a companion. But apart from that one could spend months searching through the files of any newspaper without coming across any mention of maneaters in Africa. Yet natives are being killed and eaten by the brutes nightly in some part of eastern or central Africa all the time.

This Mandimba-Mangochi area is seldom free from maneaters for more than a few months at a time. For a year to pass without news of maneaters is considered unusual. The population is entirely Muslim. They do not carry spears. Their only arms are tomahawks and knives.

To give you an idea of what they have to put up with here the following may help:

I was camped on Lake Namaramba on Portuguese territory close to where the Mandimba flows into the Lugenda at the latter's source at the toe of the lake. My good lad Aly has his home on the British side of the border in this bad area. He had been to visit his folks and when he returned to me told me that five maneaters had been ravaging the district there. The District Commissioner had sent a rifle-armed policeman, a native, to do what he could. Some local native produced an ancient muzzle-loader—probably quite illicitly-owned—and volunteered to accompany the policeman when he went out after the maneaters. One night when the moon was full they encountered all five of the lion. Good shooting on the part of the policeman accounted for three of them; whilst, incredible though it may seem, the hero with the muzzle-loader slew another! The fifth got away. Then a few months later Aly paid his folks another visit and again when he rejoined me told me that that same native policeman had been sent to the same district again and had shot another two maneaters. There had been three of them this time; but one had escaped. Then before that year was out a distant relative by marriage of Aly's was killed and eaten by another maneater, this time a solitary one.

It appeared that this woman and her husband had been visiting some relatives in another kraal some miles away. These people being Muslims do not touch alcohol; but, of course, there are always a few who do. History does not relate whether or not this woman and her man had indulged; but I am inclined to think they must have done so, or at any rate the woman had, because it is a little difficult to understand otherwise what follows. When they came to return to their own home it was already getting dark. There were two ways they could have taken: the shorter one would take them by a seldom-used path through the bush and grass, the other, much longer, by a somewhat wider and frequently-used path through a number of other kraals. An argument arose as to which path they should follow: the husband insisted that the more frequented path would be much safer, even though longer; but the wife said she was tired and sleepy and wanted to take the shorter and more direct way through the bush. Finally, since neither would give in, they decided to separate. The man followed his choice of route and the woman hers. It is this that awakens the suspicion that she must have had a few drinks, because it is very unusual for an African woman to go anywhere on her own like that, especially through the bush at night, even though she would be following a path. Then to add to the suspicion is the fact that all indications next morning showed that she must have lain down for a sleep en route.

And that was where the maneater found her. It is quite possible that she never knew she had been grabbed; there was no sign of a struggle having taken place. When the husband got home he expected to find his wife there before him, since hers had been the shorter way. Early next morning he went out to look for her, accompanied by several men from the village. It was generally supposed that she had merely slept out. But when they came to the place where she had evidently lain down, they saw a lion's pug-marks and blood. They followed for the short distance necessary and there found what the lion had left of her. They saw the lion only a short fifty yards or so away, lying in a small clump of longish grass that had somehow escaped the fires. They immediately sent one of their number to call a white man who had a tobacco plantation a few miles away. The white man came out with a rifle. The lion was still there; but the white man was so nervous that although he fired two shots he missed with them both! An ex-askari (native soldier) took the rifle from him and shot the lion dead. Strangely enough the lion had made no attempt to depart until the ex-askari had taken over the rifle, and even then he merely stood up and offered a perfect broadside shot.

There was one man here who had a remarkable escape from a maneater. He was a great big fellow, a good six feet tall, which is very unusual in central Africa where most men are inclined to be short and sturdy. He was well-proportioned and had a very deep voice. I doubt if he would ever have won a beauty competition, but when I met him he was simply hideous. He told me that one hot night he and his wife had been sleeping outside on a mat, as had the other members of the kraal. He had placed his little tomahawk on the ground at his head. Some time during the night a lion had come and grabbed him by the face and started to drag him away. He was unable to shout but his feet-kicking had kicked his wife in the face. She woke up and in the light of the moon saw what was happening. Instantly she grabbed the tomahawk, ran after the lion and walloped him over the head several times with the little axe. He was so surprised at this unexpected attack that he dropped the man and made off. The woman's yells and screams had awakened the rest of the villagers who also came running and shouting. The lion did not feel like tackling so many of them and cleared off.

The victim's face was terribly crushed. One could see where the long canines at the corners of the lion's mouth had sunk right in deep, but by some miracle they had not entered the brain pan. Nor had they injured the optic nerve. But the unfortunate man's face was a ghastly sight. I say "unfortunate" but that is scarcely the appropriate word. There cannot be many men who have awoken in the middle of the night to find their face in a maneater's mouth and lived to tell the tale. This fellow seemed quite pleased at the whole incident. Far from feeling embarrassed at his appearance, he seemed to be proud of it. He roamed around the country now both by day and by night, utterly without fear. As he loved to tell everyone he met:

"What, scared of lion! I! Why, no lion can kill me. Didn't one try? But I'm still here!"

It was extremely brave for his wife to do as she did to save her man's life. But she didn't seem to think she had done anything remarkable. When I spoke to her about it she merely smiled, shrugged a chocolate shoulder, and replied:

"He is my man, *Bwana*. I am fond of him. I could not let the lion take him. Besides, I had no time to become frightened."

When I made a very tentative reference to his appearance she just smiled the same gentle smile as she murmured:

"What does it matter, *Bwana*. He is still my man—isn't he?

His heart is still the same. He can still love me. I can still love him."

And yet there are those who will tell you that the African doesn't know the meaning of the word love. . . .

Another woman whose husband was working in Rhodesia was sleeping in her hut in another kraal with her two small children and her infant. A maneater tried to get in past the reed door. By the light of the small fire burning in the hut she saw him. She picked up a jungle knife or slasher and swiped the lion so effectively on the nose that with an astonished roar he withdrew. I killed that same brute a few days later and the proof of the woman's statement was apparent in the deep wound which had cut right through to the bone.

But it certainly is strange how some people seem to get singled out for attacks by maneaters. I have described elsewhere how a stranger who came visiting me was taken one night although he was actually sleeping closest to the glowing embers of the fire. In fact, there were two of my fellows sleeping on the same mat with him and one of them awoke to find the lion actually standing on him in order to get at the stranger. Moreover, there were about thirty of my servants and porters sleeping in pairs all around, yet the lion had walked all around them to get at this particular man. Why? That was the same maneater who had passed up her opportunity of taking my little cookboy, Friday, only half an hour previously when he went out into the forest to relieve himself. She had had a perfect opportunity to take him, yet had not done so.

Then in the Mangochi district a maneater broke into a hut and walked over two children and reached across their mother to grab the husband.

On another occasion a native youth was swooping down the hill on his bicycle to cross the bridge over the Mandimba. Quite possibly he had no brakes and was unable to stop or, since it was almost dark, perhaps he did not fully realise what he was seeing. There were two lions right on the edge of the bridge, one on either side. They merely stood there and gazed at him as he swept between them. His face must have been a picture, with his eyes out on stalks, when he was close enough to see what they were and realised that he couldn't stop! They were maneaters and they sprang on another cyclist shortly afterwards and killed and ate him.

On a small dry-season side road a party of three came face-to-face with two lion around a bend. The lion gave them the right of way; yet about twenty minutes later they took one of a party of five who were following. The spoor showed that they were the same two lion. They could scarcely have worked up an appetite in a mere twenty minutes.

Then there was a grand little fellow I knew. He was one of the small sons of the local headman on the shore of Lake Namaramba. He and I were great friends. He was such a bright cheery little chap and so intelligent and capable. He was only about twelve or thereabouts; but he kept his mother's pot well filled with fish and birds he caught and snared. One evening he was fishing in his canoe right alongside the shore of the lake. A maneater came and stood looking at him for we don't know how long. The youngster had his back turned to the lion and knew nothing of its presence; yet the lion, as his spoor showed, could have almost reached out a paw and taken him. He turned away and moved off, and scarcely ten minutes later he killed a woman who had come to draw water about twenty-five yards away.

It took me a long time to get that brute. It was very difficult country in which to hunt a single lion at that season before the grass was dry enough to burn. The local natives made it no easier; they would persist in trying to burn it long before it was ready in their attempts to drive out the cane rats and kill them. These things make quite good eating and the locals apparently get tired of their constant diet of fish. But they would make much better bags if they would wait a bit longer. With this coarse grass if it is burnt too soon, the fire just sweeps through, burning off the leaves but leaving the long strong stalks still standing. This is foul stuff through which to try to make your way; the stalks are hardened by the fire and make a fiendish noise as you battle along; they trip you up and when they break they are hard and sharp. These sharp ends stick into your legs and arms—and if you are not careful into your eyes— and when you pull them out they invariably leave a piece of their burned skin in the wound. You cannot get it out because when you try it crumbles into ash. Such wounds are very liable to fester and form tropical ulcers. Before the grass is properly burned it is almost impossible to spoor any animal smaller than an elephant (there are no rhino or buffalo on this side of the lake), and quite out of the question to track an unwounded lion.

The villages are comparatively large but widely separated. This meant that a maneater would sometimes remain in the vicinity of one of them for several days instead of following customary maneater practice of moving off elsewhere immediately after killing. The result was that when news of a human kill reached me I had to go there and do the best I could. As it would take me a full day's trekking, and sometimes two days, to arrive at the scene I was sometimes too late. The lion would have moved on and there would be no further news of him for some days. Then away I would have to go again. It took me five strenuous weeks before I finally got my shot. This time I had outguessed him and was camped in a kraal where I calculated he was due to put in an appearance.

It was just on sundown when an elderly fisherman and his son came ashore. They were taking their catch out of the canoe when the maneater appeared and took the old fellow. It just so happened that he was ashore and the son was handing the fish to him, the son being still in the canoe. As soon as the lion had carried his father into the surrounding grass the young chap raced up to the kraal to tell me. It showed great presence of mind on his part, not to say courage. I suppose most boys in similar circumstances would have been inclined to push off in the canoe until they considered they were a safe distance off-shore and then shouted for help.

I went down with him and then very slowly and quietly made my way into the grass which was shoulder-high. I had only gone about ten yards into the grass when I could clearly hear the lion feeding. Another few steps and I could see him. He was so busy feeding that he never saw me. I shot him from a range of about ten feet. I could not see him from any farther away, at least not sufficiently to be able to place my bullet where I wanted it. I think he realised my presence just a split second before I squeezed the trigger, because he had stopped feeding and it seemed that he was about to turn his head around to look in my direction.

There is something queer about this maneating. There is a big maned lion which has been living on the slopes of a kopje just back of Aly's home. He has been there for years. He comes around regularly and helps enormously to thin out the bush-pig which come raiding Aly's crops. He never attempts to interfere with Man. We often hear his sing-song roar soon after dark as he starts out for his night's prowl, and again just before daybreak when on his way home again. He seems to be a confirmed bachelor because we have never heard more than the one voice up there, and have never seen any spoor along with his. But although he comes through the lands which run right up to the village and frequently kills pig in them, he has never made even so much as a face at any of Aly's folks, much less threatened them. I feel sure it was he that Aly and I met one night when we came over the border on bicycles en route to Aly's home. We met him on that same bridge I mentioned a while ago, over the Mandimba, about a mile and a half or two miles from Aly's village. He made no attempt to interfere with us, and naturally I wouldn't dream of interfering with him. He just looked blandly at us as we passed. Aly told me that he had met him there on another occasion when it was just dusk. Aly was alone, but the big fellow acted in just the same manner. It is evident that he can live quite contentedly on the bush-pig which abound about here, so it is a little difficult to understand why the other lion that arrive from time to time cannot also do so. Or rather, will not.

I had an unpleasant time with three maneaters one night in this district. I had taken a prowl along a small side road on which people had been killed several times recently. I do not know where these lion came from or where they usually lived because I could only hear of them killing along this road. There was always considerable traffic along it—by which I mean native traffic. There would be men and boys making their way to the lake either to fish or to buy fish and sometimes their womenfolk bringing them meal. Then there would be long strings of porters toting loads of tobacco away down to Quilimane. But the killings were very irregular. One would have expected them to be much more frequent in view of the number of natives constantly passing, although the tobacco carriers, of course, would only be passing at a certain season and then later returning. But most of the killings took place when those tobacco porters were not passing. The only way to contact the brutes seemed to be to prowl along this road in the late evening and again at night.

On the night in question I had started out from camp with five new cells in my shooting lamp. I was, I suppose, about three miles along the road from camp when I suddenly felt certain the maneaters were close. I had not seen a living thing on four legs up to this time. But now, just when I felt that inner certainty that danger threatened, my lamp commenced to dim, and it continued to dim at a frightening rate. The cells must have been old stock that had been sent up here to palm off on the unsuspecting natives. It was not the first time I had been let down like that through buying cells locally, but it was the first time it had happened when I was out after maneaters.

There was nothing I could do now except turn around and retrace my steps to camp. It was a pitch dark night, heavily overcast. I think those were the longest three miles I have ever covered. All the time until I was within about half a mile of camp I felt that the maneaters were close. Then quite suddenly that feeling left me. I knew that for some reason, best known to themselves, they had turned off the road and made into the bush. But they had been following me for fully two and a half miles and I knew it. The following morning I went out and sure enough there was their spoor. I went right along to where I had turned back the previous night and found that the maneaters had been coming through the bush towards the road. They had joined the road about ten or twelve yards beyond the place where I had first felt that inner warning. My lamp had petered out entirely within but a very few minutes of the time it started to dim. I trust I shall never again find myself in a similar predicament.

I managed to kill these three eventually. Needless to remark, I did not again attempt to hunt them with locally-bought cells; but having obtained some from Blantyre in Nyasaland I again commenced my nightly prowls along that same road. As there were a number of long straight stretches on which they would see me coming for a considerable distance if they happened to be on the road themselves, I made a habit of walking along without switching on my lamp. I relied upon that infallible inner sense to warn me should I get close to them, either just around a bend in the road, or if they happened to be coming through the bush, as on that former occasion, or were just lying in the grass beside the road and waiting for someone to come along. Though I did not think that the last was very likely because people seldom walked along here by night. Most people tried to get to their destination before dark, whether or not there were maneaters about. For that very reason, of course, I could not be too sure that I would encounter them by night; but there was that never-to-be-forgotten night when they most certainly had been stalking me.

The actual killing of them was quite different to the killing of any other maneaters I had ever shot. I had strolled along the road for a few miles until once again I felt certain they were close. There was a bend in the road here so I advanced to it and switched on my shooting lamp. And there they were about thirty yards away and coming towards me. They halted when the beam of the lamp fell on them. I swung up my rifle and killed one; but the others gave me no chance at all. The instant I fired, they whipped around and bounded into the grass. It was so unexpected that I was taken completely unawares. Expecting them to offer me at least one more easy shot, I was quite unprepared for such a sudden bolt. I advanced to where the two fugitives had disappeared but the grass was too long and I was unable to see anything.

I switched out my light, lit a smoke, and deliberated on what I should do next. I wanted those two. The killing of one would probably not be enough to stop the maneating. That these had not played according to the book was only corroboration of what I well knew: that you cannot lay down hard and fast laws or rules for any wild animal—and lion have ever been the most unpredictable species. A score may act in a certain manner and then the twenty-first do something quite different, even the exact opposite of what you expected. However, it was on the cards that they would return sooner or later to see what had happened to their mate. At all events I reckoned it was worth a trial. So I strolled along the road so as to get well down-wind of the dead lion. When I was about half a mile away, I sat down with my back against a tree and lit a pipe. And as I smoked, my thoughts were at first on the maneaters: if they returned to their dead mate and I found them there— would they stand for the light? They had showed themselves so unusually shy that they might not give me a shot. And I wondered just how I ought to go about it. Then I turned my thoughts to something else. The lion could wait until I contacted them; it would be time enough then to decide when I actually saw them.

I finished my pipe, knocked out the ashes, and put it in my pocket. I was just about to get to my feet with the intention of drifting back to the dead lion when I again felt that certainty that the other two were close. It was entirely unexpected. I had been so sure that they would return to the dead one that it simply had not occurred to me that there would be the slightest likelihood of their coming around here. Yet they definitely were here somewhere. I had experienced that inner warning far too often to be deceived. It was now a question of their whereabouts.

The night was too dark for me to see any distance except along the road, the surface of which was sandy at that point. The open forest behind me only grew short grass between the trees and bushes, but it was too dark for me to see anything there unless it was very close. It was because of that short grass that I had sat me down here. Had the grass been long, danger would have been right on me before I could see it even with my lamp; but here the lamp could be used. However, I did not want to use it until the maneaters were close, lest it send them away again before I could get a shot. But not only were they close, they were getting closer. The sense of danger was becoming more and more urgent. And then I felt impelled to look over to my left. That, then, must be the danger zone.

At the first intimation of danger, I had as a matter of course, pushed forward my safety slide. I switched on my lamp at the same time as I turned my head to the left. It would have been inadvisable to have looked first. If I was being stalked by maneaters, and they were as close as I felt these must be, the very fact of my looking towards them might well have precipitated an instant attack before I was ready to meet it. But now the beam of my shooting lamp sprang out and lit up the pair of them about fifteen or twenty yards away. They were looking straight towards me.

My rifle came up and I shot one slap in the centre of the chest as she raised her head. She collapsed with a grunt and lay still. At the shot the other crouched as though she intended to attack; but I felt sure she would not have done so—I could not imagine a lion attacking anything it was unable to see. I swung my sights on to her but the instant before I squeezed the trigger she spun around and bounded away. I was following her with my sights though I had no intention of shooting unless she stopped and offered me a very much surer shot than she was offering then. After she had bounded perhaps another fifteen or twenty yards away from me, she stopped and turned broadside-on to look back and see what her pal was doing. It was what I was hoping for and my bullet drove through her shoulder, killing her where she stood.

It might be asked, how did I know that these were the three maneaters? And the answer is that I have never felt that inner warning of danger when about to meet ordinary "hunting" lion. For the simple reason that there *is* no danger then if you don't do something foolish or interfere with them. I have many times met lion face-to-face at close quarters when armed with nothing more formidable than a walking stick. But after their natural curiosity was satisfied they went their way. Furthermore, in that fine buffalo district to which I often refer, I used to have two of the magnificent big buffalo-killing lion come right past the foot of my bed night after night on their way down to the water-hole. They would stand there within not more than eight or ten feet of the foot of my bed, looking at me sleeping there. The prevailing breeze would be blowing from them to me, yet not once did their close presence awaken me. But their pug-marks would be there to tell their story next morning. The fact that this inner premonition of imminent danger does not operate under such circumstances is proof positive that there *is* no danger.

It is strange how those unaccustomed to these wild animals seem to be imbued with the notion that they will, one and all, attack man at sight. There never was such a fallacy. It can safely be stated that no wild animal will wantonly attack man —that is, without provocation. Admittedly, the provocation does not have to be yours. Somebody else may have provoked it by either clouting it in the ribs with an unsuitable bullet, or driving a poisoned arrow into it, after the poison had deteriorated until it could only cause the wound to fester. It is just too bad if you happen to encounter that animal at close quarters and without warning. But such encounters are very rare and far, far less likely to happen than an unpleasant encounter in the traffic in any large city nowadays. If you only realised it, death is much closer to you in those cities than it is in the African wilds. But you never give the traffic second thought because you have been accustomed to it all your life. And the same exactly applies to the African or to those who spend their lives in the African bush.

I fully realise, of course, that a book like this is very apt to give a false impression, dealing as it does with the unpleasant side of things out here. But I have taken that risk both because

I feel it is high time someone told of what the Africans have to put up with, and because I wish to dispel the commonly held belief that the professional hunter is a mere slaughterer. Man, irrespective of his colour, is surely of more importance in the general Scheme of Things than any animal. It is all very well for the stay-at-home arm-chair conservationist to bemoan the killing of large numbers of elephant and buffalo; but he might alter his views if he had to put up with them and found one morning on awakening that they had utterly destroyed his entire year's food supply for himself and his family! At present he has only to phone to his butcher or his grocer to have whatever it is he needs delivered at his door; but the African has no telephone and there is no butcher or grocer waiting to oblige *him*. It is only the professional hunter who can help him, If those animals had nothing else to eat there might be some excuse for them; but there is no shortage of their natural food if they will take the trouble to go and look for it.

It might be asked: Then how did the African manage in bygone days before the advent of the white man? Why not let him carry-on as he used to do? And the answer to that, is that in the first place, there were fewer Africans owing to inter-tribal wars, epidemics, and constant and incessant slave-raiding. Their lands therefore were not nearly so widespread as they are today. Then, secondly, he used to kill many elephant annually but, of necessity, his methods nearly all resulted in a lingering death to the elephant. How different is the clean instantaneous death inflicted by the experienced elephant-hunter. The African is not permitted to kill elephant nowadays even if they are raiding his lands—which seems grossly unjust if the government will not send a hunter along to help him. Because the Africans are my friends, I have always felt fully justified in killing elephant, buffalo, hippo occasionally, crocs and maneating lion.

K

The Maneaters and Lion-Men
of Usori

USORI in Tanganyika is another of those very bad districts. At least it certainly used to be. I have not been there for a number of years now and it is possible that there have been great changes since the last war. But it used to have a very bad reputation.

I first heard of it back in 1922, I think it was. At that time the District Commissioner, the Assistant D.C. and another white man, either an Agricultural Officer or a member of the Veterinary Department, went out, sometimes together, sometimes separately, to see what they could do to help. But it was long before they had any success. One of their main difficulties was the power of the witch-doctors. There was what amounted to a guild of them with one reigning supreme, a kind of Grand Master. These men claimed and always had claimed that they could transmogrify themselves into lion at will. It goes without saying the locals all implicitly believed in them, and it also goes without saying that the witch-doctors played on that belief and profited by it. Instead of threatening to curse someone, as witch-doctors elsewhere might do, these men told their intended victims that they would be killed and eaten by a maneating lion. And since the villagers firmly believed that the witch-doctor could change himself into the form of a lion whenever he wanted, they had no hope of escape. The lion would know where each of them lived and where and when to lie in wait. Such were-lion would naturally have the intelligence and knowledge of humans, since they were actually humans in animal form. Stiff payments in cattle and goats and occasionally money were demanded by the witch-doctors to ward off the calamity. Some of these witch-doctors were known—they made no secret of the fact. But there were others and nobody but the "Grand Master" knew who they were. They worked for him like a secret police force or Intelligence agents. Bad and all as the actual maneaters were, these "Lion-Men" were feared far more. That was just the trouble: the natives could not be brought to believe that the maneaters were real lion—they invariably insisted they must be some of the witch-doctors. And here is where the Grand Master showed his cunning. Had he not had his secret helpers it could have been proved to the villagers that the maneaters were indeed lion by having all the known witch-doctors under observation when there was an attack by a maneater. But since the entire district could not be kept under observation, the witch-doctors had it all their own way.

Some remarkable coincidences took place while those whites were actually there. And it is, of course, coincidence that keeps superstition alive. For example, on one occasion they followed the spoor of a very big black-maned lion which was said to be the leader of the pride of maneaters. They followed until they came to a great slightly rounded piece of rock forming a small hill. Naturally, they lost the spoor here as the rock would not hold pug-marks; but they cast around the edge of the rock until directly opposite where they had lost the lion's pug-marks they found the foot-prints of a man continuing in the same direction, and nowhere could they find any more lion pugs. Their native trackers assured them that the big lion had merely changed itself back into human form.

Then on another occasion after they had arrested a witch-doctor and shut him up in a hut, the wizard broke out of the hut and ran across the open space in the centre of the kraal. As it was bright moonlight, everybody saw him. There was a concerted rush to grab him because he was an acknowledged "lion-man", had boasted of the fact loudly to the white men and assured them they would never be able to hold him. He disappeared into the long grass that bordered the kraal but just as the villagers reached the grass only a few moments later, they met a big lion which roared angrily at them. They fled, quite convinced that the wizard had changed himself into a lion again as he had boasted he could and would. The white men arrived on the scene soon after and were shown the tracks of the fleeing wizard. They were then shown the pugs of the lion which had appeared close by only a few moments after the man had disappeared in the grass.

The white men's explanation was that the man had apparently spotted the lion in time to shin up a tree and was actually up the tree and probably watching the consternation of the villagers when they came face-to-face with the lion. He must have been congratulating himself at his luck to have such a fortuitous coincidence occur just then. His reputation would receive a tremendous boost.

It can readily be appreciated how incidents such as the above would merely serve to increase the locals faith in the ability of the different wizards and witch-doctors throughout the area. They were averse from helping the whites and had to be persuaded to do so. They had disliked the idea of locking up that wizard, and were scared that if they helped the whites to kill the maneaters, the other witch-doctors would be on to them for helping to slay one of their number. Naturally, the witch-doctors wanted to have maneaters around because they were such useful tools. If there were never any maneaters around, the natives' faith in, and fear of the witch-doctors would have been greatly lessened. As some of them, especially the Grand Master, were becoming extremely wealthy by East African standards for those days, that would never do. The witch-doctor's main asset, like that of the priest of bygone days—and even of today—is the fear he can build up in the minds of his people. It matters not if the fear is of some dreadful physical harm that will be suffered here and now in the near future; or whether it is some hideous retribution that will be inflicted by-and-by after death.

There was another strange thing about these maneaters, and that was that there seemed to be at least one mob of five or six led by a fine black-maned lion. And that is most unusual. Such beasts seldom take to maneating except in the case of one that had been wounded and left or lost. But in that case, he would have been solitary. And once again there was no good excuse for them to take to maneating. There was plenty of game for them had they wanted it, if not there then not far away.

But the belief that some men and women can change themselves into animals at will, is literally universal. In Africa it may be into lion, leopard, crocs or hyenas; in Australia, into dingos, crocs or cockatoos; in Canada and Europe, into wolves; in India, into tiger, leopard (panther), hyenas; in Egypt, into jackals; in South America, into jaguar; in England, into hares; in Eire, into IT, which is so horrible that it has no name and is indescribable. This is without doubt among the most widely-held beliefs on earth; and since many of these different races had no contact with one another until recent times, how is it that this same belief is held by all of them? Surely it can only be explained by folk tales from the remote past which *must* have had some basis in fact, no matter how distorted they may have become through the centuries. At any rate, since it is only the day before yesterday that the English peasant firmly believed that some people could change themselves into hares at certain seasons, the African out in the bush can scarcely be held up to

ridicule for his firm conviction, when he sees strange coincidences around him, that there are those who can change
themselves into maneating lion. (There was one coincidence I
might mention that came under my own observation: a very
decent old headman I knew was accused of changing himself
into a maneating croc so that he could eat his own children.
A big maneating croc had appeared in the lagoon of Lifumba
where no maneating croc had ever been known in the memory
of the oldest greybeard—and the African has a very long
memory. The man was put to the poison ordeal, unhesitatingly
drank the poison while stoutly protesting his innocence, and
was dead two hours later, thereby conclusively proving his
guilt. As further proof there was the indisputable fact that the
maneater disappeared and was never seen or heard of again.)

Those whites shot some of the maneating lion—I forget how
many—and arrested the Grand Master and a couple of lesser
wizards and sentenced them to a term of imprisonment. As
the Grand Master was led away he vowed vengeance on the
villagers of his district when he returned. But since that would
not be for some years, the locals put it out of their minds.

It was somewhere in the thirties that I happened to be
passing through the Usori district. I camped there one night
and the natives told me that they were again being troubled
by maneaters. That was nothing unusual for them; but there
seemed to be more of them than ever and they were again led
by a big black-maned lion. They felt certain that this must be
the Grand Master again. Nobody quite knew where he was:
some said he had died in prison; others, that he had been
released a year or two previously and was lying low, though
they did not know where. They all remembered now that he
had vowed vengeance on them for helping the whites to arrest
him and for giving evidence against him. There had been
maneaters in the district during the intervening years, but

nothing like so many as there were now. They knew of the
big pride, the one that was led by black-mane, and it consisted
of five or six beasts; but there was also another lot of
three or four. Sometimes there were a pair and occasionally
a solitary one. These may or may not have belonged to one
of the larger parties, but they did not think so. If not, it would
mean that there must be at least eleven of the brutes in the
district.

Of course, some of them were undoubtedly witch-doctors;
but they were now quite prepared to believe that some were
genuine lions. They could remember that some "real" lion
had been killed that other time by the whites and an occasional
one since. Nevertheless, their belief still held that some were
were-lion—as witness the fact that the whites were unable to
kill many of them in spite of their rifles. They had all fired a
number of abortive shots as was only to be expected if they
tried to kill a were-lion. However, they asked me if I would
stop over for a while and help them, promising me all the
assistance they could give me. Naturally, I agreed to do so.

It was the greatest number of maneaters I had ever had to
tackle. All members of the cat family have one trait in common:
they do not poach on each other's hunting ground at the same
time. That is to say, if one party is attacking a certain kraal:
any other maneater(s) in the vicinity will not attack that same
kraal at that time or even that night: they will move on elsewhere. Whether this was going to make it easier for me, or
still more difficult, I did not yet know. But it would inevitably
mean considerable moving around as it would be impossible
to refuse to answer an urgent S O S.

I had a number of porters with me in addition to my
personal servants, cook and gunbearers. The villagers could not
possibly find accommodation for them all, and in any case, I
considered they would be safer in camp with me. The common

belief that fires will keep determined lion at bay is entirely erroneous, and the same applies to thorn fences. But in my experience, and I have had a lot of experience in maneater country, pressure-fed storm lanterns will. The most common size is of three hundred candle-power. If you have not too many men one of these will do: put it on a box or something and then have your men all sleep around it as though it was a fire. They will be quite safe so long as you train yourself to wake up just once during the night in order to pump up the lamp as the level of the kerosene drops. When I had a larger number of porters, as on this occasion, I would hang several of these lamps around the sleeping circle. I have never had even the most determined maneater venture into that dazzling blaze of light. My men knew this and were quite content to remain in camp with me.

We had just got the camp fixed to our liking for the night when we heard some men and women shouting and yelling about a hundred and fifty yards away. They were on the path that led to the water. These people were so accustomed to maneaters that they invariably went together in parties. This must have been a party of women who had been down to draw water and would be accompanied by a number of men armed with spears and axes. But these were primarily agriculturalists and not hunters: their spears were very different from those carried by the Masai. It was bush country with plenty of four-foot grass all over. I might mention that if, as was customary, the women had been washing themselves as well as drawing water, the men would have withdrawn to such a distance that they would still be able to act as guards but not able to see the women. The African is very particular about such matters. There are no "Peeping Toms" amongst them. Even amongst the completely nude tribes, men and women do not bathe together.

My gunbearer and I hastened along the path to where we met the party. The men told us that several lion had approached close to them in the grass, but since they were in a compact group with no stragglers apparently the lion did not feel like attacking. They were unable to say with any certainty how many lion there had been; but at least three—some thought more.

I at once entered the grass where the lion had been seen. It was evident that several animals had recently moved through it. It was impossible to see any tracks; but it was easy to see that several creatures had pushed down or pushed aside the grass. It could have been men, but it was almost certainly the lion that had been seen. Unfortunately the grass prevented me seeing them because it became longer as I advanced. Finally I was compelled to abandon the chase.

But that night we heard the drums from another kraal about a mile away, so out I went with my gunbearer. From the noise being made as we approached the kraal, it would seem to be a determined attack. But I did not actually see it because before I reached the scene of the attack, a lion stepped out of the grass immediately in front of me. I take it the brute was on its way to join the party and did not know of my existence. It was little more than twice its own length ahead of me when it appeared on the path; it had its head turned away from me, looking in the direction of all the noise. Naturally, I had my shooting lamp switched on, and when the lioness—it was a female—noticed the strong white beam she looked quite casually around towards me as though wondering what the moon was doing so close.

I shot her and hastened along to the kraal, hoping to get there in time to bag some of the others. But my shot must have scared them, because all noise had stopped instantly when I fired, and when I arrived, there was not a lion to be seen, though I wandered around swinging the beam of my light in all directions.

It was strange that these beasts should be so nervous. In my experience, maneating lion are not inclined to be so. Admittedly, maneaters had from time to time been shot-up here to a somewhat greater extent than they had in most other parts of Africa with which I am acquainted; nevertheless, the local natives had told me that no one had hunted them here for a considerable time. I could only hope that they all would not prove so, or it would make my job very much more difficult and take me a great deal longer to clear the district. (And that last was a matter of some little importance, because technically I had no business to be there at all: that is, I had no licence to hunt in Tanganyika—I had merely been passing through. Although you might think that surely no official would object to my hunting maneaters, with or without a licence, unfortunately that is not always the case.)

Although I had only managed to bag one out of this lot, there was no need to be disappointed—the night was still young and those that had been scared away would still be hungry. It was probable that they would make another attempt before dawn somewhere else. And either they or another lot did very shortly after my gunbearer, Nasib-bin-Risik, and I had returned to camp past the dead lioness.

We heard the drums beating in another kraal in a slightly different direction and immediately started out. We had only about a mile and a half to go and long before we got there we could hear the terror-stricken yells and screams of the unfortunate people. Things were in a bad way here. There seemed to be lion everywhere. There was one up on a roof immediately in front of me trying to tear its way in through the thatch. I shot it, and it tumbled to the ground with a snarling roar. But I was confident of my shot and anyway could not attend to it just then even if it did need another bullet. Two more of the brutes emerged from a hut right beside me when they heard the shot. They were only nine or ten paces away. I killed both of them also without any trouble. (As I later found, they had broken down the reed door and killed all the occupants of the hut: an old grey-haired woman and three little children.)

But that was not all. Such appalling screams had been coming from another hut on the far side of the kraal, that I was convinced another tragedy must have taken place there. The yelling and screaming everywhere had ceased as soon as I fired the first shot; but over there it had seemed to continue for just a moment longer, and there had been an unpleasant choking sound immediately before it stopped. I made my way over there, swinging the beam of my lamp on each and every door and roof. At last I saw what I had feared: a broken down door and a gaping hole in the thatch of the roof.

Naturally assuming that the killers would have departed I walked straight towards the open doorway to see if there was any life left amongst the occupants. But, as a matter of course, I was carrying my rifle ready for immediate use as I stopped to enter the hut. And it is a good thing I was; because whilst I was still stooping and only halfway into the hut, peering around the reed door which had been pushed to one side but had only half fallen, I found myself face-to-face with a big lioness with another as big beside her and, immediately beyond them, a magnificent black-maned lion. The nearest of them was a mere five feet away. The interior of the hut was like a slaughter-house. There were five dead girls and the lion were busy feeding on them, the hard mud floor a sea of blood.

I could not take all this in immediately. I realised that the maneaters had killed and saw that huge pool of fresh blood. I had to make up my mind without delay just what I was going to do. Had we been outside in the open it would have been perfectly straightforward and had there been only one, or at most two, of them in the hut it would not have needed much thought; but I had never tackled three of the brutes before under such conditions. I knew I could kill two—but what was that third one going to do? I knew that animals will seldom attack something they cannot see, and, of course, these would be completely dazzled by my lamp. All the same that third one would know it was trapped here in the hut and might well be expected to make some kind of attempt to break out. And then, even as I opened fire, I remembered that big hole in the roof: at least one of them must have broken in through it and so I could only hope that if any of them tried a break when I commenced shooting, they would try it that way and not out of the door past me. There wasn't room for a lion to get past me, and I had no hankering to be brushed out of the way by any lion.

It is really remarkable how long it takes to describe one's thoughts during such tense moments—thoughts that whip through one's mind quite literally with the speed of light.

The nearer lioness stood up as I stuck my head in, but her two companions continued to lie there on the bodies of the slain. Accordingly, I killed her with my first shot: at a range of five feet there could be no question of missing. At the shot, I saw out of the corner of my eye, black-mane leap for the hole in the roof. I could do nothing about it. The second lioness had jumped to her feet, but since she had been looking towards me probably did not know that the big fellow had made his break. I had no difficulty in killing her because she merely stood there gazing at the light and then down at her sister, doubtless wondering why she was taking no interest in the goings-on.

I regretted losing the big black-maned leader of this pride as I stood there looking at those five dead girls. The eldest of them might have been sixteen or seventeen years of age. Even so horrible a death could not disguise her beauty—she was an exquisite creature by any standard: her features, her eyes, her lovely young breasts that required no artificial aids.

But black-mane had gone. I followed the direction in which he must have fled—as my gunbearer, who was immediately outside the hut whilst all this had been going on, would otherwise have seen him. And it was very fortunate that he had broken in through the roof other than immediately above the door, otherwise he would have come straight down on my man's head. Still, that would have meant that he would have had to jump right over me and my light, which was not very probable.

The wretched villagers' delight at the slaying of five of the maneaters was badly offset by the deaths of so many of their own members. And on top of that was the further certainty that the black-maned leader of the pride could be none other than the great wizard himself. Otherwise, how explain his escape when he was actually in the hut with the rifle which had just killed his two wives and three of his companions? It *could* only be a were-lion. And then inevitably someone remembered that last time, the big-maned leader of a pride had never been shot. It goes without saying that when news of all this got around the district every witch-doctor and wizard confirmed the general belief. It was useless my attempting to assure them that black-mane was just another lion which would one day fall to my rifle if he continued maneating. What does a white man know about such matters? They were much too well-bred and polite to say so to me, of course; but I know the African and know that dead-pan expressionless look of which he is such a master when he drops that curtain back of his eyes. The white man is without doubt, very clever with his guns, his cars, his airplanes and such; but what does he know about witchcraft?

And once again things seemed to favour this belief in the
were-lion. He killed again and again in different parts of the
district. I shot other maneaters here and there, but never a
glimpse of that black-maned brute. I bagged a party of three
one night after I had shifted my camp some miles away.
Maneating certainly fell off around there where I had killed
those six (including the first one); but there was still all too
much going on elsewhere. The reports that there was a lone
black-maned maneater still on the job was borne out by his
pug marks which I had very carefully examined. I was able to
recognise them on several occasions. However, it is possible
that the reports were exaggerated through fear, since the
ground was such that it was not always possible to identify
the tracks of a soft-footed animal—one could just see that it
had been a lion and that was all. Support for this came when
I succeeded in killing a lone maneater, a big lion, in one of the
places where there had been reports of black-mane but where
I had been unable to identify his pugs. But the locals would
not have it: they merely informed me that this was some other
"real" lion, and thanked me for hunting it down and killing
it—but, of course, I could never kill black-mane because black-
mane *wasn't* a lion. It was very good of me to try and they
much appreciated my efforts on their behalf; but I was really
wasting my time now that I had shot and killed so many
genuine maneaters. Ten—wasn't it? No hunter had ever shot
so many before in this district.

But that black-maned brute had put me on my metal. He
had become, I think, the deadliest and most determined, and
the most fearless, maneater I had ever hunted. Whereas
previously, when leading his pride, he had not attacked by
day when meeting with an armed party, now that he was alone
he began to do so. Admittedly, the arms these poor people
carried were mainly to boost their own confidence when

threatened by lion. They would have been little better than useless had they actually been attacked, at any rate by more than one maneater. Though usually maneaters, like "ordinary" lion leave the actual killing to one of their number, that does not always hold good, especially at night. For example, when cattle-killers cause a mob of cattle to break out of a kraal—a favourite game of theirs—they will frequently kill several beasts, presumably to make sure they have enough. A determined bunch of maneaters will also sometimes make individual attacks—like that pride led by black-mane that night. But it is most unusual for even so feebly-armed a party as these were to be actually attacked by day even by a pride of maneaters. Yet here was this bad brute actually attacking and killing them all by himself. The entire district was becoming so demoralised that there was much talk of emigrating right out of it. Then others pointed out that that would be quite useless since there was nothing to prevent the chief wizard in the form of this lion from following them, no matter where they went.

It was a bad show. The people had to go to the water: the grass was not yet ready to burn: nobody knew where the maneater was going to turn up next: he seemed to know quite well that parties from every kraal in the district would be going to the water every day at some time or another: he had only to be patient and they would come past his ambush. His method was to spring out on the last member of the party, as a rule, and be away with him into the grass before the others fully realised what had happened. And they just dared not follow him into that grass when so inadequately armed. I said that was his general rule and what one would have expected of a maneater making a daylight attack; but there were occasions when he showed his utter contempt by taking either a man or a woman from any part of the line. And on account of the grass and bush the people were compelled in most places to walk in single-file. They could seldom keep in a compact bunch.

I tried everything I knew, everything my long experience with maneaters had taught me, to contact this brute. But he seemed to bear a charmed life. Of course, the advantages were all on his side: he could come and go as he pleased, attack wherever he wanted to. And, like most maneaters, he usually travelled considerable distances between kills. It was quite impossible to outguess him and get to some likely place where he *might* be expected to make his next attack: he was much too irregular. I found it equally useless to set a trap for him and bait it with myself, as I had done with considerable success elsewhere in the past. He seemed to have almost completely given up night attacks—apparently he was finding his daylight assaults so much easier and successful, so much more certain.

Much and all as the local natives had wanted me to help them, and much and all as they would have liked to be free of this scourge, I found they were no longer anxious to help me. On the contrary, they seemed anxious for me to move on out of the district. The reason being that they were now positive that that chief wizard was punishing them not only for the past but for having me here now to try to kill this were-lion. And their main fear was that if I stayed any longer, the witch-doctor would either blast me with a curse or, more probably, have his were-lion kill and eat me. And they were scared of what the authorities might do to them in either case. All this meant that I had great difficulty in getting any reliable news of the maneater now.

Then almost quite by chance, I not only got the news I wanted, but was able to kill the brute and prove entirely to my satisfaction, and that of my gunbearer, that it was indeed the black-maned leader of that pride and also the lone black-maned maneater which had been terrorising the countryside for so long.

And yet it was not quite by chance. It was due to my friendship with two of the youngsters who spent most of their time in my camp. They were locals who had come to visit us after I had shifted my camp for the third time. They were just two African Negro youths; but two of that type you will find here and there all over the world, irrespective of race or colour, who are instantly attractive: bright-eyed, cheery, intelligent and willing, they were very fond of one another and were always together. I had liked them as soon as I saw them and they seemed to know that instantly. They were very friendly and liked to sit close and watch me and chat if I wanted to chat. They knew perfectly well that I was not being given all the help the locals might have given me, and that those locals—their own people—actually wanted me to leave the district. In fact, it was principally through them that I knew all this. Then one day they told me they were going out to look for wild honey: a honey bird had been around inviting them, and they were going out to see what he had to show them.

The honey bird is one of the most remarkable and pleasing features of the African bush. He will come around your camp and start calling immediately, flying from tree to tree to attract your attention. The African, knowing him so well, just goes about whatever it is he is doing, taking absolutely no notice of the little fellow. But that in no way discourages him: he waits for a short while and then re-commences his excited calling and fluttering around. When they are ready and not before, those who want to follow him collect whatever they are likely to need and whistle to the little bird to let him know they are ready. He becomes greatly excited then and flies off to another tree not too far away, all the time twittering and calling. So it goes on until he arrives at the hive. Here he flutters from branch to branch, incessantly calling and twittering until he sees his followers have commenced operations.

L

He thereupon flies to another tree close-by and just sits there watching—not another chirp out of him. But should the men consider for any reason that that particular hive is unget-at-able, they whistle to the little fellow and at once he starts off towards some other hive he knows about. He does not appear to be the least bit put out. I might mention that it is not the honey he wants but the comb with the young grubs in it. So it is customary for the men to leave him a little of that. He does not seem to mind how little it is; he is always willing and ready to lead them or anyone else to another hive. He would seem to have an inexhaustable knowledge of their whereabouts.

And this was the honey bird my two young friends were telling me about that they wanted to follow. I reminded them of the maneater; though we had not heard any news of him for several days, he might still be anywhere. But the two lads were typical Africans and as such did not worry their heads about unpleasant possibilities that *might* happen: time enough to start worrying when danger actually approached. Besides, their eyes were bright and keen. They each had a little tomahawk; but asked me shyly if I would give them a few matches, promising to bring me some of the honey if I would. Naturally, I gave them a box of matches assuring them I was not trading them for honey or anything else: if they found plenty, I would certainly be grateful for a little, but they were not to run themselves short on my account. So off they went.

Less than an hour later they came racing back into camp and, their eyes dancing and sparkling with excitement, gasped:

"*Bwana! Bwana!* The black maneater! He's eating something over there! It was when we climbed up the tree to see about the honey that we were able to see him. He doesn't know we saw him. If you come quickly, Bwana, you can shoot him now."

It was enough for me. Grabbing a rifle, I told them to lead on.

They led me to the tree to which the little honey bird had guided them. He must have been disappointed that they had run away so soon after arrival and without showing any more interest either in that hive or any other, because there was no sign of him. One of the lads climbed up, had a good look in a certain direction, grinned down at us, and pointed, nodding his head to indicate that the lion was still there. Down he came then and rejoined us.

"He's still there, Bwana," he whispered. "Come; I'll show you."

We moved quietly through the rather open scrub and shortish grass for about seventy-five yards. Then my young guide halted and peered cautiously around a low bush. Instantly he froze and then very slowly, like the real bushman he was, he drew back and indicated to me to come forward and take his place. His hand on my upper arm drew me gently into position and a mere lift of his chin showed me where to look.

And there, barely twenty-five paces away, lay a magnificent black-maned lion making his toilet: licking one forearm and rubbing it over his whiskers and face, like the great cat he was. (And what a job a good-maned lion must have after a meal! He seems to be a very messy eater.)

He never heard the rifle and never knew what killed him. It was as easy as that.

It was an old man he had been feeding on. Only the old fellow himself could explain what he had been doing all by himself so that nobody knew he had been taken—and he would never speak again. There was little left of him now.

A careful examination of the pugs and the tracks round about proved conclusively that this was the dreaded "were-lion", the transmogrified wizard.

My two young companions were delighted. All shyness

they might normally have had disappeared and they grasped me by the hands and patted me on the shoulders, completely forgetting the essential part they had played in the death of this dreaded killer. But I reminded them of it and assured them that the entire district would know also.

I then suggested that we go get that honey and asked them to whistle up that little honey guide—he probably wouldn't be far away—for surely he also deserved his reward. If it had not been for him we might never have known that black-mane was so close and so vulnerable. This suggestion pleased the two lads greatly. And sure enough they succeeded in calling up a honey guide. Of course there was no telling if it was the same one or another; but we like to think it was the original that had led the boys to this hive. And really the idea is not so far-fetched as it may seem to the stay-at-home: most creatures, animals, birds and fish, have chosen areas for their hunting and living generally and will chase away any intruders of the same species. In all the years of my wanderings in the African bush I cannot remember ever having had more than one honey guide lead us at the same time, or seen another around when we were robbing the hive.

Do I need to add that the local natives refused to believe that the dead black-mane was really the bad lion? It would be quite impossible for anyone to kill a were-lion. However, the maneating stopped abruptly throughout the entire Usori district with the killing of that brute. I had estimated that there must be eleven in the district if all the accounts I had received were accurate—and this was the eleventh I had shot. That he was a maneater was indisputable; and his pugs were easily identifiable.

But the locals insisted that the chief wizard had tired of maneating for the time being, and that this just happened to be another "real" lion.

The Ankwazi Maneater

FORTUNATELY maneating leopard are very rare in Eastern and Central Africa, but once they start they are very much worse than lion. They are worse and much more dangerous because they seem to be more cunning and definitely more fearless; moreover, they can climb where no lion would even attempt to climb. They are much quicker than lion and far better camouflaged. On top of all that is the appalling damage they can do in a matter of seconds due to their custom of using all four sets of claws in addition to their teeth; whereas a lion is inclined to use his claws merely to hold while he bites. A leopard can rip a man literally to threads, to ribbons, in a very few seconds. The damage done has to be seen to be properly appreciated or even believed.

When you remember that the ordinary "hunting" leopard will think nothing of entering the room in which you are sleeping to take your dog or anything else that may take his fancy—though he is not likely to interfere with you—you will realise that when he chooses to become a maneater he has none of that natural fear of human habitations to overcome that the lion has. And this also shows that he really does not fear man at all. The ordinary leopard will keep out of your way by day—you will seldom see one in daylight—but that is merely because he is not looking for trouble, not because he is scared of you. It is also, of course, because he is much more strictly nocturnal than the lion. But you certainly will not find lion wandering through your tent or bedroom unless he is definitely after you.

The leopard has another unpleasant trait which you do not find with lion: the fact that he will frequently kill seemingly just for the pleasure of doing so—as all-too-many men will. . . I admit that this is mostly seen when a leopard breaks into a goat kraal or sheep pen; nevertheless, I have also known maneating leopard kill far more than sufficient for a feed. Yet on other occasions I have known the brute take one of the occupants of a hut without the others knowing anything about it until the following morning.

In all the many years of my wanderings in Africa, I have seldom been called upon to hunt down a maneating leopard.

There was one extraordinary case that took place on the bank of the Zambezi about halfway between the town of Tete and Nsungu at the upper entrance to the Lupata Gorge. I was hunting elephant at the time on the other side of the river. Natives told me that a leopard had broken into a hut across on the north bank and had killed an old woman in it. Since I knew that that stretch was often bad for maneating lion, and since I had not then ever heard of a maneating leopard, I figured it must have been a lion. But I was assured that the pugs were too small for a lion, in addition to which spotted hair—or rather hair of several colours—had been found where the beast had forced its way through the thatch of the roof. However, I also knew that the lion of that area were inclined to be small and also held their cub spots much longer than was customary, almost until they were adult. In fact, I have shot fully mature lion there on which I could clearly see the spots, especially on the belly, when the sun struck the hide at a certain angle.

However, I crossed the river to see what I could do. Once there I had to admit that my informants were entirely correct. There was no doubt whatever, that the damage had been done by a big leopard. But the extraordinary thing about it all, was that that leopard was never heard of again! He just made that one killing and disappeared. And what is more, there did not seem to be any reason for it since he seemingly made no attempt to eat the body of the old woman: he just forced his way in through the roof, killed, and then jumped out again through the hole he had made in the thatch. Though I think he may have drunk the blood—there seemed to me to be surprisingly little about. But is it any wonder that superstitions live when such things happen without apparent reason? At least not what you and I might consider reason. To the locals, of course, it was all quite obvious: some witch or wizard had trans-mogrified himself into a leopard for the express purpose of killing the old dame, as was conclusively proved by the fact that it did not kill anyone else and had no existence after killing the old woman. They just could not understand why the white man had to make it more difficult for himself by refusing to accept such an obvious explanation and searching day after day, and night after night, for a non-existent creature. And non-existent it certainly was, at any rate as far as I was concerned and seemingly as far as anyone else was concerned because, as I said, it was never heard of or seen again.

But by far the worst was the brute that became notorious as the Ankwazi maneater. Ankwazi is a pretty big district on the north side of the lower river—that is, below the Gorge. And from Bandari at the lower entrance to the gorge right along the river to Ankwazi itself, and then throughout the many scattered kraals lying back from the river and up to Sweza, just south of the Nyasaland border, was ranged and ravaged by this very big leopard. His favoured part seemed to run from the river and up along the east side of the lagoon of Lifumba as far as Sweza. But curiously enough he never crossed the British border into Nyasaland, although there was an even more densely populated district there.

I first heard of him when I came down to Lifumba one year for my annual war against the buffalo herds which did so much damage to the local natives' food crops. For several years it had been my custom to spend four months or so there during the season when the buffalo joined up into those immense herds which were capable of such devastation. I was told of a big leopard which had been playing havoc throughout the district during the rains. He had killed many people, men, women and children, and had mauled a number of others. Several of these last were brought to me so that I might dress their wounds and see those whose wounds had already healed. These were the lucky ones. Many others had died of their wounds.

I asked if they were certain that people were actually being eaten by the leopard, and not merely killed by him and then eaten by hyenas and similar scavengers. Because I knew that leopard will occasionally take to man-mauling for no apparent reason: a leopard will without warning rush out of the surrounding bush or forest, terribly maul some unfortunate woman or girl or man or whoever happens to be there in the lands, and then decamp without making any attempt to eat its victim. I have no explanation for this extraordinary conduct which, I am glad to say, is somewhat rare unless it is some kind of rabies. But I am not qualified to discuss that; and there is no getting away from the fact that I have never heard of any of the victims developing the disease.

But it was with this in mind that I queried the men; because such a man-mauler is a very different thing from a maneater. From what I had seen of it and heard of it man-mauling did not persist: it seemed to die a natural death after running its course. Which would seem to strengthen my conviction that it must be some kind of disease or series of fits—like those which will make a domestic cat race around and around the room, even to dashing around the walls like those stunt motor-cyclists riding their "Wall of Death". I do not know if it was the disease which died out after running its course, or whether it was the leopard that died after a cumulative series of such fits. It is useless to ask if I never found a leopard dead from unknown causes in a district in which there had been an outbreak of man-mauling. One seldom finds a dead animal in the African bush. Vultures, hyenas, jackals, ants, take care of that.

The local men assured me that there was no doubt whatever that the leopard was a maneater, but there had been no news of him for the past few weeks. When I asked how it came about that some of the leopard's victims had only been mauled, they explained that these people just happened to be there when the brute made his attack. Under such circumstances he would sometimes savagely maul everyone in sight before carrying away one of them. The speed of a leopard's attack is almost incredible and I could readily picture it all happening just as the men described it. On other occasions, as when for example there was a party walking along a path, the leopard in true maneater fashion would pick off the last man after allowing the others to pass unmolested.

Throughout the months I was there hunting buffalo, there was no news of the maneater, and I not unnaturally thought he had gone or had met with his end in whatever way leopards do meet with their end. Accordingly, when the buffalo left the district with the first rains, I as usual, also left.

Elephant occupied me for the ensuing seven or eight months; and then I again returned to Lifumba for buffalo. To my surprise I learned that shortly after I had left the previous year, the leopard had returned and re-commenced maneating. I had been much too far away up the river for any news of these parts to reach me. I had been hunting amongst different tribes and the Lifumba people never came up here, neither did these people ever get so far down river as to hear of the leopard. Anyway, they would have had no interest in what might have been happening around Lifumba to people of a different tribe.

It always occasioned me wonder that the different African tribes had so little interest in neighbouring tribes. It all dates back, I suppose, to the days—not so very long ago—when they were in a perpetual state of war with one another. If not open war, then inter-tribal raids. And yet, is it so very different from conditions among the civilised tribes of Europe? One might be excused for supposing that the exalted white rulers consider it too crude merely to jab an assegai through one's enemy's liver; in these "advanced" days nothing less than the wholesale devastation of atomic weapons is permissible. . . .

However, once again the leopard disappeared; and there was no sign of him during the four months I was there. But I saw where he had been. There were certain trees he much favoured. These were worn quite smooth where he so often sprang or climbed up to lie out on a branch from which he could see a considerable distance along some path. In each case there was a small bush growing at the foot of the tree; and it was quite obvious that when he saw some travellers coming he would drop down and ambush them from behind that little bush. Unquestionably, leopard do sometimes drop down on their prey from some overhanging branch; but in my experience they much prefer to ambush from the ground. I do not forget that long ago I had a leopard drop down on me from an overhanging branch, as I have described elsewhere; but I do not think he was actually ambushing me so far from all human habitation. Had he been a maneater he would have been closer to where he could expect to find his favourite dish. At any rate, this brute certainly preferred to drop down from the tree prior to attacking. The ground told its own story as clearly as any book; as also did the tree.

This year I might have stayed there after the buffalo left; but I had already received a call to come to the assistance of some people that had been having a very bad time with three man-eating lion in a different district. So, since the leopard might or might not return again this year, whereas the lion were actually there in that other district, I once again packed up and trekked away.

I was sorry to go because I like these people around Lifumba and knew them as well as they knew me, whereas the other people were comparative strangers. After I had dealt with the maneaters, the elephant commenced raiding the earlier half-ripe crops, so that I was again kept busy. But this year I was not so far away that news could not reach me from Lifumba occasionally. Thus, I heard that the leopard had indeed returned and reawakened his reign of terror there.

As soon as I could get away, I returned to Lifumba some two or three months earlier than I usually did. This meant that the buffalo had not yet come down from the valleys amongst the hills, so I could concentrate on the maneater if he was still in the district.

And he was still in the district. I was horrified when I heard an account of his killings and maulings during the months I had been away. It had become so bad that many of the villages had been abandoned: the villagers just packing up and going to stay with relatives elsewhere. It had not been possible for them to build new villages and of course they had had to leave their food crops to the tender mercies of anything that cared to come raiding them. What food they had left over from the previous year they took with them. But, and it is a curious thing, as soon as the African abandons his kraal it begins to fall to pieces. You will sometimes see them living in an old hut which you would think would collapse any moment; but they have been living in it like that for years, and without doubt could continue doing so if they wanted to, or were too lazy to repair it or build a new one. Let them leave it, however, and it will fall down almost overnight. I cannot adequately explain it; but you will see it to a somewhat lesser extent with ships.

Many, indeed most, of these kraals had been in good repair the previous year and right up to the time I left the district just a few months previously; yet now it was pathetic to see the ruin everywhere. Only two staunch families had refused to leave. They had been the first families in the district—at least their ancestors had—and they were determined that no leopard or anything else would drive them out of it.

To a great extent this should have made it that much easier for me to contact the brute, because if he wanted man now, he would have to come to one or other of these families. Except, of course, for the two well-travelled paths running through the district and meeting at right angles down on the river bank: the path coming down from Sweza and the road from Bandari to Ankwazi. The riverain folk were still there because the leopard had only made occasional sorties amongst them: it was the area between the river and Sweza that had suffered most.

Leaving my canoe-men on the little island in the lagoon where I had had a base camp for several years, and whereon they would be perfectly safe and could get my precious vegetable garden going again, I and my "flying squad"—six young strong fellows game for anything, plus my cook and the youngster who helps him—made our way to the camp I customarily use during the buffalo-hunting season, as it is central and easily reached by anyone coming with news.

The leopard was still in the district and still killing. Several times perspiring runners arrived in camp to tell me that someone had been killed and eaten. Invariably I would go with them; but it was sheer waste of energy. Mostly the country was covered with long "buffalo" grass; but where the grass was shorter the ground was covered with small stones over which it was utterly impossible to spoor a soft-footed animal. In some of the kraals they had built leopard traps; but they had proved useless because the people had nothing with which to bait them. (It was all tsetse-fly country so that they had no domestic animals to use for that purpose). They had just built the traps in the hope that the leopard might be sufficiently curious to enter, and so trap himself. But he had not done so. It did not occur to any of them to use themselves as bait, and bearing in mind how poorly they were armed I cannot blame them. Having used myself as bait for maneating lion several times in the past, I knew just what it was like—and I was armed with a powerful rifle.

But it seemed that there was no other method I could use here with any hope of success, at any rate until the grass was burnt. Then, if the brute followed his usual custom, he would clear out of the district. I could not help wondering where he went during those months. Certainly he was not maneating elsewhere or I should have heard of it; and yet he had shown his partiality for human flesh to such a marked extent throughout each of the last three rainy seasons that it was more than strange that he should be so apparently willing to switch back to a normal diet each year. That is very unlike usual maneater custom; in fact, it is a complete reversal of it.

Of course, it was all witchcraft—all such visitations invariably are; but it was strange that not once did I hear a suggestion that it was a were-leopard. I had expected to be told so; but to my surprise they seemed quite sure that it was just a bad leopard which had been bewitched into maneating by some wizard who had a "down" on the district. There always had been many leopard in the district—one heard their sawing nightly—but nobody had ever bothered their heads about them because it had hitherto been unknown for one of them to interfere with Man.

The kraal to which I had been called had a leopard trap built on the outskirts just where the path led in to the clearing. I sat in it all night in vain. It had not been at all pleasant because the builders had only made the one compartment. They had seen no object in making a second compartment since they had no goat or other bait to put in it. And I had arrived too late in the day for any alterations to be made.

It had been an old man who had been taken this time. He had been visiting from a neighbouring kraal some three miles away. There had been two of them and the maneater had taken the second one as they walked single-file along the path, without the one in front, probably only a pace and a half or at most two paces away, knowing anything about it! When walking along like that the African talks all the time, but without ever looking round. It was only when the old fellow had practically reached the village and had asked his companion some question for the second time without getting any answer that he looked around to see why. Then he found that he was alone. Thinking that his old friend had stopped to relieve nature before arriving at the village, he waited for a while and doubtless followed, as he thought, his friend's example. But when there was still no sign of his friend he began to get a bit worried. As the village was so close he hastened along to ask someone to come with him to look for his friend. About a mile away they found the old fellow's blanket and, at the side of the path, his light spear. The pug marks of a big leopard told the story. They went back to the village for reinforcements in order to recover anything the leopard might have left of the victim.

From what I have seen of them, maneating leopard in Africa will kill just as readily by day as by night. Jim Corbett says that in India the people feel, and are, quite safe from maneating leopard during daylight hours. That certainly does not hold good for Africa—which is a little difficult to understand because I have been told by zoologists that there is no difference between the African and Indian leopard. (In some parts of India they are called panther, but there is no difference apart from the name.)

I returned to my camp and awaited further news of the leopard. He had preceded me along much of the path; and where the ground permitted, I was able to examine his great pugs: they were almost as big as those of a lioness—by far the biggest leopard pugs I had ever seen, or for that matter, have ever subsequently seen. There would be no difficulty in identifying them at any later stage.

He had passed my camp—which was empty—and had continued on in the direction of the river. The following morning my gunbearer and I followed the same path to where there was one of the trees he so much favoured. I wondered if I would have any success were I to climb up either it or another, about thirty yards away and wait for him to come along, since I now knew he was somewhere around in these parts. However I was not very optimistic because there was comparatively little foliage on any of the trees just there: I would be very conspicuous. One must never forget that leopard look up into treetops because baboons are their favourite food. Lion, on the other hand, do not look up. In addition to which, the leopard I was after would naturally look up into his own tree before climbing. Of course, it was my hope that I would spot him coming before he was close enough to start looking up. Against that was the difficulty I would have in seeing him in the long grass. In fact, there was really no chance of so seeing

him. I would only be able to do so if he crossed the road or
came a short distance along it before reaching the foot of the
tree. As I looked around I saw that it would have to be his tree
or none. From none of the other possibles could I see enough
of the road surface to get a sure shot even if he did come along
it.

So, since I could not risk my gunbearer by sending him
back to camp all by himself, the two of us climbed up into
the leopard tree. This actually was a good thing because my
companion could then keep a lookout on my "blind" side.
Otherwise I would have to keep turning all the time, and that
would have been inadvisable.

The day dragged by but there was no sign of the leopard.
We abandoned our perch in time to reach camp before dark.
Next day we tried the same thing on another of the maneater's favourite trees, but without avail. It was very disap-
pointing: but there are always many disappointments when
hunting maneaters, especially under such difficult conditions
of long grass and stony ground where the grass was short.
There were no stones at all here in this part, but the grass and
the ground baked iron-hard by the sun, effectively prevented
any chance of spooring a leopard.

After several fruitless days without news, we got word of
an attack in a kraal along the river. Some women had been
down to the river to wash and draw water and were returning
to their huts. As usual they were walking in single-file along
the path. Without warning a big leopard sprang out of the
matetti reeds, through which they were passing, and grabbed
a little girl of about twelve or thirteen years of age who was
almost in the centre of the line of women and children. Her
mother was immediately behind her with a large earthern pot
of water on her head. As her little daughter went down under
the leopard, the mother, with great presence of mind, dashed

the heavy pot of water down on the leopard's head and neck. The pot shattered with the impact; but the attack was so unexpected and so surprising that the leopard sprang away into the *matetti* and disappeared.

You would think that the brave mother surely deserved better of Fate, or whatever you like to call it; but the little girl's neck was broken and she was dead.

All that night I prowled around the kraal and backwards and forwards along the different paths leading to the water and to the lands in the hope that if the maneater was still around I might contact him. But having that heavy pot full of water—it would have contained four or five gallons of water, and if I remember rightly, four gallons weigh forty pounds, while the pot itself is no featherweight—smashed down on his head proved too much for him. It is a fact that he never again came around this kraal or this far up the river. Although the mother lost her daughter, she without doubt saved the lives of several other people who might otherwise have been killed around here. I doubt, however, if that knowledge would have seemed much comfort to her or consolation for the untimely death of her little girl—and such a lovely little child she was. . . .

The leopard was next heard of some five or six miles farther down river, so down we went after him. Here we found that three little boys had built themselves a small hut about twenty feet above the ground in the convenient fork of a large tree that grew on the outskirts of their village. It was not built as a safeguard against the maneater, but boys the world over will build such a little hut for their games. They had taken to sleeping in it and this night the leopard had come, climbed the tree without waking them, and had killed them all without anybody in the huts of the village knowing anything about it. The leopard had then fed and afterwards decamped. It was

M

only long after sun-up when the boys did not show up that their parents wondered why. There was no response to their calls to the boys. Then one of the men went over to the tree and there saw the pugs of the maneater on the bare sandy ground at the foot of the tree.

Since it is a regular custom of the ordinary "hunting" leopard to cache the remains of his kill in the fork of a tree to protect it from hyenas, and since the maneater had left so much of this kill up in this tree—the greater part of one boy had been eaten, but the other two bodies were untouched—it seemed likely the brute might return that night for another feed.

The people had left things just as they discovered them until I arrived. I now told them they could remove the bodies of the two boys that had not been eaten, but asked them to leave the remains of the other. I promised them that the remains would not be interfered with because I intended to sit up with them myself in the little hut in the hope that the maneater would return. They were rather shocked at the thought of me sitting in the little hut all night with such grizzly company, but did not argue. There was no accounting for white folks: they did the most extraordinary things and flouted all omens without thought. Nothing on earth would have induced any of them to sit all night with the remains of the unfortunate lad, and in the dark at that!

There was a half moon that night which would set about midnight. It was getting near the horizon before I heard what I had been listening for: a light scraping on the trunk of the tree. It could only be the leopard climbing up. The boys of course had had a ladder of their own construction as a permanent fitting which I had used; but no leopard would use it. I had banked on hearing his claws on the tree because I failed to see how he could climb a vertical tree in absolute silence.

He certainly did not make much noise—not enough to awaken a sleeper who was not expecting danger, as those poor lads had not been expecting it. They doubtless considered they were perfectly safe up here in their eyrie. But I had been listening for just such a noise as I now heard. Moreover, immediately before I heard it I once again experienced that inner warning of danger which told me that my quarry must have arrived. There was nothing urgent about the premonition. I was awake and had a shotgun loaded with $1\frac{1}{4}$ oz of buckshot in my hands and would have a leopard at a considerable disadvantage since he could only claw his way into the little hut comparatively slowly. In other words, I was in little real danger.

The scraping sounds came closer and closer and then stopped. For a moment there was absolute silence and then I saw a dark solid shadow pass the openwork sides of the hut in order to reach the open doorway. Next instant a leopard stuck his head into the doorway and I fired point-blank into his face, the muzzles of my gun not more than three or four feet away from him. He disappeared and I heard a thump from the ground under the treetop hut. The instant I fired, I scrambled to the doorway and looked down just in case the brute had not been killed outright, though I had little doubt. He was there and he made no move.

I climbed down the ladder to find myself surrounded by the villagers, to whom I had called out, to tell them that the leopard was dead. There was great joy amongst them; but I felt a sick feeling flow through me when I more closely examined the dead leopard. Even as he stuck his head into the open doorway, I had thought it seemed small for an animal with such immense pugs as I knew the maneater possessed, but of course I had had no time for more than a glance the very instant before I squeezed my trigger; but now the dead leopard lying there on the ground could not possibly be the maneater that had been playing such havoc throughout the district for the past three years: it was much too small. Quite a good sized leopard, but not such an outstanding animal as the maneater must be. This one's pugs could never make such tracks as I had followed along the path that day, and which I had seen again at the foot of the tree on arrival at the village here the previous day.

I tried to explain all this to the villagers; but they would not have it. Wasn't the kill up in the tree? Didn't this leopard climb up to the kill? Didn't he stick his head into the doorway of the little hut? Of course it must be the maneater.

I reminded them that leopard will take an easy feed if they can get it just as lion will. My explanation was that this leopard happened to be prowling and winded the remains of the dead boy up in the tree. He had then merely climbed up to see if there was anything for him easier than hunting it on the ground. I was so convinced that I had not shot the maneater that I spent the remainder of the night up in the little hut. When the maneater did not put in an appearance, the locals were more than ever convinced that he had been shot and that I had sat up needlessly. I could not agree with them, much and all as I should have liked to. Daylight showed even more fully that the dead leopard could not have made the pug-marks made by the big maneater; his paws were much too small. Another of those sickening disappointments.

Of course, any leopard I spotted or encountered by night was suspect and had to be shot. There would be no chance of identification until after it was dead. By day it might be possible, but in this district one practically never saw a leopard in daylight, so that if a leopard *was* seen it would almost certainly be the bad one.

And then, just when the entire district was beginning to sigh with relief at the lifting of the terror, came news of another human kill! It was what I had feared: what I had been certain of. I *knew* the maneater was still at large.

When the word flashed around and through the district that I had shot a leopard which had attempted to climb into that little hut up in the tree where the three boys had been killed, in typical African fashion most of the inhabitants of the district immediately relaxed all precautions. The result was inevitable: a man well known to me had gone out to tap some of his trees for palm wine. He had gone alone and spent the day out there, drinking the wine as soon as enough had run to make a drink. He had probably had a skin-full by sundown and was on his way home carrying a calabash of wine when the maneater pulled him down. Nobody worried when he failed to return to the kraal that night—they took it for granted that he would be out in the palm grove, sleeping off a good drunk. But when someone went out the following forenoon to join him, taking some food along, his calabash was found and also some blood and the pug marks of a big leopard.

They sent for me and I hunted around there for several days; but saw nothing of the maneater. Again and again I tried sitting in a leopard trap, using myself as bait, but this brute, seemingly, had no interest in such traps or was too wise to enter them.

Two months had rolled away by now and the buffalo started coming down from their hill valleys as the water and mud dried up there. This now was the only area big enough for their numbers and holding sufficient water and that all-important mud for baths and wallows. Buffalo become so verminous that life must be miserable for them if they cannot wallow in good wet mud pretty frequently. Once again the maneater disappeared.

For the next four months I was busy amongst the buffalo; but when they left the district after the first heavy rains, I stayed on. For a couple of weeks nothing happened, and then came news of another human kill. The maneater had returned. Conditions now were a lot easier because all the long grass had long been burned off, and those first heavy rains had slightly softened the surface of the ground so that it was possible to spoor the maneater to some extent in places. Furthermore, I could use my shooting lamp to a vastly greater extent than previously, when the grass had rendered it useless except actually on a path. During the next two months, before the grass grew too long again, I shot seven leopards by night, hoping that each one might be the bad one. But they proved but another seven disappointments.

Then one day after the grass had again grown shoulderhigh, I went out some three or four miles to shoot some meat for my men. I did not want the maneater to hear my rifle speak anywhere in the immediate vicinity, lest it warn him that I was still there, because he seemed to be much more cautious this year than he had been before. It was just possible that he knew there was danger here this year.

My gunbearer was breaking trail through the grass until we came to where we knew there was shorter grass and to where I expected to get the shot I wanted at some little impala. We were approaching a lone tree shaped like an open umbrella. The trunk was quite bare and the foliage very dense. It was perhaps fifteen to twenty feet high. There was little or no grass immediately under the tree, giving a clear circular space about ten yards across surrounded on all sides by the ocean of long grass through which we were trampling. As we came to the tree, I thought absently to myself that it would make a perfect lying-up place for a leopard; but I never dreamt for an instant that the maneater would be out here so far from human habitation at this time of the year when he was again on the rampage. But I had only taken one step on to the clear patch when I suddenly felt an urgent impelling sense of imminent danger. I had been carrying my rifle carelessly on my shoulder, muzzles foremost, because now that the buffalo had gone I had not expected to meet anything in the long grass. I had come out for impala, and I knew that they never entered long grass. I swung my rifle down from my shoulder and got hold of it in two hands and shoved forward the safety catch. This could only mean that the maneater *was* somewhere close. He must be in that tree which had looked such a likely place for a leopard. I had taken a couple of paces forward whilst getting my rifle ready for instant use. I now halted and looked up carefully into that dense foliage to see if I could spot the leopard. And that did it. He of course, had been able to see us coming. Had we merely passed beneath him he might have allowed us to go if he had not been hungry—and it was in the last degree improbable that he was hungry or he would not have been lying up there: he would have been hunting, as he had long shown that he had no objection to hunting Man by day. On the other hand he might have been deliberately ambushing us with the intention of dropping down on the last man to pass under him. I had several of my men with me to carry back to camp whatever meat I shot.

A leopard will often allow you to pass quite close to him if he thinks you have not spotted him, but the instant you stop and look towards him he dashes away. Even if when walking, your eye catches his, he disappears. And so it was this time: the instant I stopped and looked up into the tree there was a rush in the foliage and a great dark shadow passed between me and the sun and disappeared in the grass. Just as it disappeared, I got a glimpse of a leopard's hindquarters—they were almost as big as those of a lioness. I have never before or since seen such a gigantic leopard, even though it was but a glimpse I had of his backside.

There had been no time for even the quickest of snapshots. The brute had leaped right over my head, and I had had to turn right around in order to see him as he landed right at the edge of the long grass. It had all happened so quickly, far, far quicker than it takes to describe, that my rifle was only half way to my shoulder by the time he had gone.

I feel certain he would have tried to grab the last man to pass if I had not stopped like that. Had it been otherwise, I do not think I would have felt such an urgent warning. But it had been absolutely imperative.

It was rather strange that this brute which had shown such utter contempt for Man, and which thought nothing of hunting him by day, should nevertheless act in such a typically leopard-like way when he realised that I had stopped and was looking for him. It certainly was not fear. I take it, it was just his natural reaction, his natural reflexes which took immediate control and caused him to beat an instant retreat.

If only that foliage had not been quite so dense I would probably have spotted him before we reached the little clearing and I might have been able to shoot him. But that is the way it goes.

I knew it would be sheer waste of time and energy to try to track him through that ocean of grass. He would not stop in it; but would continue right along until he came to more bush. So I went on my way and collected the meat we needed in camp.

It was several days later before we heard of him again. It seemed that he had pulled down one of two youths who were returning to their home from the river where they had been fishing. The one in front was carrying a fish spear. This consisted of a straight length of round iron without any barb, stuck into a shaft of light bamboo. It is used solely for impaling mud fish (or cat fish—sometimes called barbel) which the fisherman feels with his bare feet. Having jabbed the spear through the fish he can reach down and get hold of it. For its purpose the spear is entirely adequate; but it is a poor weapon for use against a maneating leopard. Yet this youth swung around when he heard the leopard spring on his pal, and without hesitation threw his fish spear into the brute. He then ran for help. Judging by the tracks the leopard was too busy biting the shaft of the spear and trying to get it out of his flank, to chase after the fleeing boy. It was an exceedingly plucky thing to do, but that is very typical African behaviour where a friend is concerned.

The tracks showed that the leopard had spun around several times and we found the spear shaft well chewed by the animal's teeth. There was a very slight blood-spoor which I followed for several miles, but it was only an occasional drop and soon petered out. The wound, though slight, had been sufficient to drive the leopard away so that the body of the boy's friend had not been eaten.

For another month or six weeks I hunted the brute in vain. And it would be nice now to tell you how I finally managed to slay him—and as in fiction I would have to; but I am not writing fiction and the truth compels me to admit that I quit everything and went off to the war. . . .

N

The Mangwendi Marauders

THIS was an exceptionally determined herd of elephant raiders. There were about sixty or seventy animals in the herd and they came raiding the food crops year after year. Several times I had tackled them by night when actually raiding; but had only shot one or two each time: one can seldom bag more than that at night. This had merely had the effect of driving the survivors a few miles away to continue their depredations in some other lands. It was obviously necessary for me to teach them a lesson, a lesson they would not forget for many a long day. These were not direct mankillers; but they had been responsible for considerable malnutrition and partial starvation for at least three years. Killing a number of them would almost certainly have the result of driving the survivors right out of the district and teaching them that it was not only inadvisable to raid man's handiwork, but definitely dangerous. Elephant are very intelligent and can learn such lessons. In fact, Elephant Control is based solely upon this premise.

I picked up their spoor and followed them for miles until I caught up with them in one of those places you dream about with everything in your favour: a fair-sized clearing in the light open forest with a mud-wallow in the middle of it and a couple of dusting places close by. Halfway between the fringe of the forest and the mud-wallow was a small anthill with a couple of forked trees growing out of it so that it was like three or four small trees. This afforded adequate cover for me and my gunbearers. The trees broke up our outline which made us invisible provided we kept still, yet in no way interfered with our view of the herd or impeded quick handling and exchange or rifles. An ideal spot. The anthill was perhaps forty paces from the mud-wallow and twenty to thirty paces from the two dusting places.

We sighted the herd when fully a hundred and fifty yards away, and I stopped to test the wind and reconnoitre my approach. The elephant were thoroughly enjoying themselves: slapping dollops of mud on to their shoulders and backs with a satisfying "clop", as happy as kids making mud-pies; others, having had their mud baths, were scraping the bare ground of the dusting places with one huge forefoot, then sucking up a trunkful of the dust and puffing it over heads, necks and shoulders, and behind huge ears, for all the world like a woman with a scent-squirt when completing her toilet. One very big bull, which I guessed was the leader, had had his bath and shampoo and was now standing doing nothing under the trees on the anthill, but on the far side of them. That was very satisfactory. Although we would be within some fifteen feet of him or thereabouts, I could see no very good reason why, if we used reasonable precautions, he should spot us until too late. Accordingly, I parked my followers at the fringe of the forest with instructions to remain there. I and my gun-bearers advanced across the open towards the anthill, keeping it as much as possible between us and the elephant.

It must be remembered that elephant have not got good eyesight and anyway do not normally rely upon their eyes to warn them of danger. They rely almost entirely upon their power of smell which surpasses that of any other animal as far as distance is concerned. It is quite unnecessary to crouch and crawl when approaching unsuspicious elephant; but it is also important that there should be no sudden or jerky movements or rapid movements. Rapid movements will alarm any wild animal because they themselves only move rapidly when avoiding danger. Accordingly, any rapid movement they see indicates danger in the offing, and so puts them on the alert.

I was armed with three rifles on this occasion: two double-barrelled, a 470 and a 465, and a Mauser-actioned repeater, a 416.

Having placed myself in position, I opened fire with the Mauser. My first shot killed the big leader where he stood. He dropped instantly and thereby gave me a clear view of the remainder of the herd. They swung around in all directions, ears out and trunks up, awaiting the signal from the big fellow to give them the line of retreat. This is the correct method to adopt when you want several members of the herd—in my experience they will almost always wait for a considerable time before attempting to flee, thereby giving you a number of shots if you want them. But it is essential to drop the leader with a clean brain-shot. A heart or lung shot will not do, an elephant will run for anything from forty or fifty yards with a heart-shot and anything up to half a mile with a lung-shot. When he goes the others will go with him. But if you have brought him down with your first shot, the remainder will be lost without his leadership, not knowing that he is dead.

I ripped off the remaining three shots from the magazine just as quickly as I could manipulate the bolt and swing on another elephant. The first to get it was another big bull directly facing me. I shot him in the centre of his great chest, just at the base of the throat; and immediately gave another, standing beside him, an identical shot. The fourth bullet found the brain of yet another good tusker as he stood broadside-on to me. The remainder of the herd appeared to be flabbergasted at this rapid burst of fire. Some of them milled around a bit, but the majority just stood not knowing what to do. Having emptied the 416, I grabbed the 470, knowing that my man would reload the Mauser without having to be told to. One bull must have seen the movement and started towards me. Whether he intended to charge or not I really cannot say. I gave him no time to make up his mind. My bullet took him between the eyes and he was dead before he hit the ground. Another that had moved forward with him swung away when he saw his mate fall, and my left barrel took him through the shoulder. He lifted that foot about ten or twelve inches off the ground, hesitated a moment, and then made as though to take a pace forward; but the busted shoulder would not take the weight and down he came. These two shots were fired so quickly that my man had not had time to finish reloading the 416, so I reloaded the 470 myself. I could have shot a number of smaller elephant now, but only wanted the big ones. The milling around had mixed them up, and although I could see several good bulls, there were cows and immature animals between me and them. So I decided to wait for a spell and see if they would open out and give me a better chance. By this time the 416 was ready, so I took it over as I liked its peep-sight when in the open like this.

There having been dead silence and no movement for some time. A number of the elephant began to get restless, as though feeling that something ought to be done. This was what I was waiting for, and raised my rifle, steadying myself against one of the little trees. Gradually the herd opened out. I had spotted the two best tuskers remaining and was all set to take the fullest possible advantage of any chance I was offered. Presently I got it. The big fellow I wanted was right away on the far side of the herd, but the movement of the others between him and me gradually exposed him. He was side-on to me and I drove my bullet through his shoulder. He stumbled and fell almost instantly. The various animals past which the bullet had whizzed had doubtless heard it "clup" into his shoulder and seen him fall.

They swung around to look, thinking there must be fresh danger from there now. It had been a long shot at elephant—all of sixty paces; but it was worth it because this turning of so many of the herd exposed a lung-shot at the other big one. As I have previously mentioned I prefer not to take lung-shots if I can help it; but on this occasion I didn't mind as I had already killed several of the bigger members of the herd and could see that I would almost certainly be given two or three more easy shots even if the herd did start to stampede now. So I let rip, and away he went. He dashed off after his trunk and the rest of the herd commenced to go too, stringing out some as they got under way.

This gave me another two shots as two more shootable bulls showed themselves. Both these were shoulder shots as they ran across my front, and both crashed in their tracks. This caused considerable confusion: those elephant close behind tried to pull up, whilst those further in the rear, not knowing what had happened, tried to push on. The 416 again being empty, I once more took over the 470.

And now I did a foolish thing—knowing perfectly well that it was foolish! The herd had again halted, and I could see two quite good bulls standing with their backs to me. Now you can kill an elephant with a clean brain-shot from the rear, provided you have the angle right and know what you are doing; but it is a very difficult shot to bring off successfully and requires nice judgment. It was quite permissible for me to take this shot, as I had frequently brought it off successfully; but it was very unwise of me to attempt it with the 470. This rifle, like all my powerful doubles, was specially sighted for close-range work in heavy forest and had an extra large foresight. It was never intended for a tricky shot like this which requires great accuracy of aim unless you are very close. These elephant were at least fifty yards away, and what I should have done was to wait until the 416 was ready and use it. Its aperture sight would have been entirely suitable. Instead, I stupidly attempted the shots with the 470. Both bulls tumbled to the ground in a heap.

I reloaded, but I could see nothing else worth shooting, so I waited for the survivors to clear off. When they eventually did so, we closed in to examine the fallen. Suddenly my gunbearer drew my attention to the fact that the last two bulls were struggling to their feet. Accordingly, I had to give each of them another shot. That finished matters for the morning; although we were not finished with elephant yet for the day.

A round dozen tuskers with fourteen shots was good going, and I was correspondingly pleased. After admiring their tusks and estimating their weights, we had a rest and a smoke before starting the return march to camp. These elephant had led us around in a great semi-circle, and we decided to cut across a segment of that circle so as to shorten the distance back to where the rest of my men were bivouacked. Even as we came in sight of them I heard something away to our left, but I imagined it was probably one of my men collecting firewood or something. However, when they caught sight of us my men ran to tell me that there had been a party of seven bull elephant around the camp all morning. They had first seen them perhaps an hour after we had left, and they had been feeding in the vicinity ever since. They were now over there where I had heard some noise a few minutes ago.

I at once made over towards them, carrying my 465. My head gunbearer was carrying the 470 and my second bearer the 416. I found the seven bulls, good ones they were too, in light open timber with a fair amount of four-foot grass about. It was easy shooting conditions. I saw that my head gunbearer had estimated the possibilities as quickly as I had, because when I took up position within some twenty paces of the elephant, who were standing close together, I noticed that he signed to the younger lad to stand close to him with the 416. The two biggest bulls were standing side-on to me, cheek by jowl, facing in opposite directions. I opened fire with the 465, killing them both with a quick right-and-left, and exchanged my gun for the 470. Not waiting to reload it, my head gunbearer instantly handed it along to the youngster and took the 416 from him. He could see that I might want all seven or eight shots quickly. I got one with a frontal brain-shot and then fired the second barrel into the chest of another. The three remaining elephant milled around and swung from side to side, but could not make up their minds what to do. With the 416 I shot two through the shoulder, and then killed the last with a side brain-shot. They were all so close together that there was scarcely room to move between them.

You will without doubt have noticed that I kill nearly all my elephant with a single shot apiece. But do not forget the close ranges at which elephant are shot. There is really no excuse for failing to kill. The secret is not to get all steamed-up and excited. Don't attempt to squeeze your trigger until you can clearly see your way to place your bullet where it will do the most good. Patience and steadiness are of vastly greater importance than marksmanship.

I have provided a shot-by-shot account of that day's hunting to give you some idea of a professional elephant-hunter's job. Of course, by no means all days are like that. Far more often than not one spends days and days hunting but a single bad raider; or sometimes one may spend all day in order to kill only one or two out of a small but persistent party of marauders. As I have previously mentioned, nobody was paying me for this work of protecting the natives' food crops or for hunting man-eating lion and similar marauders. I had to pay myself out of what ivory I happened to shoot—and all too often there was little or no ivory worth taking, especially if it was a party led by some old cow, a party which had to be discouraged and taught not to molest the crops. I was never interested in the financial side of my hunting: just so long as I was able to pay my men and keep my spare ammunition bag well-filled, I was content.

I fully realise that there are those stay-at-homes who know nothing of the actual facts, the TRUE facts, of conditions appertaining in elephant country in Africa, and who will without doubt raise their voices in shocked protest at the thought of any man slaying nineteen elephant in one day. I have shot more in a single day—my biggest bag was thirty-eight elephant: they had bogged themselves hopelessly in a swamp and I was forced to give them a quick and merciful death rather than leave them there to die slowly and miserably of thirst and starvation. On another day I shot twenty-seven elephant. I agree that these are high figures, but I was protecting the natives. I was not like those so-called sportsmen who may slaughter thousands of grouse or pheasants—birds which were not doing any harm to anybody and were actually bred at great cost for the sole purpose of being shot. Would my critics feel so tenderhearted towards those same elephant if they had to watch little children slowly starving as a direct result of the depredations of those elephant? My hunting and killing of those marauding elephant not only safeguarded the food crops. The meat of the slain animals was some compensation to the natives for the loss of their food.

In another part of this same district the natives were constantly troubled by elephant raiders. This was definitely not the same herd, because I was told that the raiding was done by one or two big bulls each time and not by any big mixed herd. I might mention that that big herd cleared right out of the district that year. It returned the next year; but there was no raiding. They had obviously learned their lesson.

This other place where the raiding was carried out by lone

bulls or pairs of bulls now occupied my attention. There was a chance for me to recoup my expenses in addition to helping the local natives. One morning I came across immense pad marks in the lands where the millet had been raided overnight, and went after them. If this fellow was carrying any ivory at all it was sure to be good stuff. Several times I sighted him; but he just would not halt. Whether he had some favoured spot in view and was making for it, or whether he was merely wandering because he had nothing else to do, I cannot say; but on and on he went. He did not hurry; but then an elephant does not need to hurry to cover a lot of ground.

The sun mounted higher and higher until it was nearly overhead. Around 11 o'clock, when we had covered about fifteen miles, the elephant showed signs of pulling up and seeking a shady spot. He was very particular, for he passed up several trees that looked good enough to me. At last he found what he was looking for. I could not see that it was any better than several others he had tried and left, but there must have been something about it that made it seem more attractive to him. Or perhaps he was just tired of the search himself. Whatever the reason, it gave me the chance for which I had so long been waiting. I had already seen that he had tusks although I had only glimpsed the tips of them, at least I knew that my long tramp was not for nothing.

The conditions were quite favourable for me. There was a fair amount of bush about, but a clear space round the tree under which he was standing. I had no difficulty in getting within some fifteen paces of him. He was totally unconscious of danger. But he was facing away from me and, as is all-too-usual around the midday hours, the breeze was becoming rather treacherous—giving every indication that it was going to start puffing from all directions. So I knew I must get my shot with the least possible delay. To move around on his left would have brought me dangerously close to the wind, whilst if I went to his right the trunk of the tree would obstruct matters.

There was nothing to do but turn him. So, with my lips almost touching my gunbearer's ear, I just breathed a word. The man slowly stooped and picked up a couple of dry twigs. Gently he cracked one. That one little sound caught the big fellow's attention. He knew he ought to be alone out here—so who or what was moving around to crack twigs? His great ears swung out, but he did not otherwise move. Again my gunbearer cracked a twig, not loudly, but enough. The big bull, and he was a monster, came slowly around, head towards the tree. I was using a Purdey double 450/400, one of my favourite rifles, and slipped a bullet into his brain when he came side-on to me. He never knew what hit him. Nothing could have been easier.

I had long known that my quarry was a mighty animal, but it was only now that I was alongside him I realised just how enormous were his proportions. He was literally gigantic—one of the very biggest elephant I have ever shot. His tusks, of immense girth, were solid ivory throughout: they had no hollows—just shallow saucer-like concavities. This indicates that he must have been very old; because the hollows only fill up with great age.

And now we had another fifteen miles to trudge to get back to camp. . . .

There was a place here in this district I determined to work, because it was clear that the old bulls which had been raiding the crops round about lived in there. It consisted of a large piece of country roughly circular in shape and with very dense thorn all around the circumference perhaps two or three miles in depth. It must have covered between 2,000 and 3,000 square miles. I had penetrated some distance into it once before during the rains when conditions are very much easier owing to the fact that a certain amount of water is then available. The local natives had told me that no hunter in the memory of the oldest grey-beard had ever attempted it. One or two people had penetrated perhaps half a mile into the thorn, but that had been enough for them.

Even the natives living around the circumference wherever there was water never penetrated far into it. There was nothing to induce them to. All they knew about it was that there was no water to be had except what lay during the rains. That information had come down through the ages. When I had previously tackled this area I had noticed from time to time some very attractive spoor around the scarce waterholes "outside", and that the makers of the spoor invariably returned to the thorn whence they had come. The local natives had been able to tell me that there were many big old tuskers in there, and that they had almost all been wounded in the surrounding districts in the past. The elephant apparently looked upon the place as a sanctuary, and a sanctuary it had been if no hunter had ever ventured into it. These old bulls do not have to water daily as the cows and calves do. They may only venture out to a waterhole two or three times a week depending on the season, and may not come out for months during the rains. Anyway, they will only do so at night and take good care to be well within their own preserves before daybreak.

It would seem, however, that long years of immunity had been responsible for some of the inhabitants of the sanctuary losing their natural healthy respect for Man: their wounds had long healed: nobody had been hunting them: it is possible they had not heard a rifle speak for many years. And so now some of them had re-commenced raiding the crops. Well, then, they would have to be punished. It would be much too slow and laborious to wait for them to raid and then follow them back through all that thorn. What I intended to do was to go right out into the heart of the "sanctuary" and then hunt them out there. It was quite time I shot a few good tuskers, as my expenses had been heavy during the past twelve months and funds were getting mighty low.

Water was a difficulty at this season but by no means an insuperable one. I am in the habit of carrying around a few 10-gallon drums in which to store flour, sugar, rice and so on in any base camp I build. They protect the food from the rats. These drums make excellent receptacles for water when away from camp.

I shot a couple of buffalo to keep my men going, and then began to go into the thorn. Every available man carried water except my gunbearer, cook, and the little youngster who helps him. For the first two or three miles the thorn was very dense, but we were following the fairly recent spoor of an elephant so that we were able to get along. There were rhino scattered about in those first three miles but not beyond that. The thorn was getting less and less dense, and finally opened out into what should have been, rather surprisingly, quite pleasant country if only there had been surface water in it. Big trees here and there indicated that there was probably water not so very far beneath the surface: but most of the trees were baobabs.

These weird vegetable monstrosities were plentiful, and it was apparent that many of them held water in their hollow trunks for long spells after the rains. We could see where elephant had reared up against them, keeping their hind legs on the ground, and reached down as far as they could with their trunks into the "tank" as the level of the water dropped. Earlier in the year these reservoirs would without doubt have kept us going since we could have drawn water from them long after the elephant were unable to push down far enough with their trunks. But the rains had been over some months now and the water had evaporated from all but the biggest of the baobabs.

We pushed on until I estimated we had covered some fifteen to twenty miles, and then looked around for a good shady tree under which to bivouac. We found this and camped down. I had brought no tent, camp furniture, or other needless paraphernalia along. The water was dumped into the drums. At daybreak next morning I and my gunbearer, cook and his little assistant, would remain whilst all the others would return. It would take them the greater part of the day to get out; so they would sleep "outside" and return the following day or the day after that with more water for us. In this way we could continue hunting almost indefinitely if there were sufficient elephant to make it worth while. We could shift camp ten or a dozen miles from time to time as seemed desirable.

We started out for a cruise around at the same time as the water-carriers left. Elephant were liable to be encountered anywhere at all here, since this was a definite feeding ground and rest home. If we struck fresh spoor I meant to follow it, but at that stage I meant only to wander around with our eyes and ears open. The big bulls that frequent such a place would not roam around more than was absolutely necessary. There would be no cows or calves here: it was too far from water.

We sighted our first big fellow within an hour of leaving camp. He was drifting somewhat aimlessly along, pulling up an occasional tuft of grass, knocking the earth off its roots against his knees, and then sweeping it into his mouth. He did not appear to have much interest in what he was eating, and it rather looked as though he was doing it much as you or I will pluck a stem of grass, chew it for a few moments, and then spit it out. There was no breath of air stirring and, save for an occasional tree or small bush, no cover. But the big bull was utterly unconscious of danger—in all probability a rifle had never been fired in here since the world began. I walked slowly forward so as to intercept him. I stood waiting beside a small bush about four feet high.

I was again using my 400. The elephant never saw me. He drifted slowly along perhaps fifteen paces away; and I slipped my bullet into his brain. Just the one shot, and then silence settled down again. Other elephant in the vicinity would not be alarmed. They would doubt their own ears if they heard the report of a rifle. It was unprecedented: one didn't hear rifles in here, they must have been dreaming, or else it was another elephant smashing a tree. We cut off the tail of the bull and left him there.

About an hour and a half later we spotted another two elephant. They were standing under a tree in the centre of an open patch. They were both big, but one was an enormous brute. A little breeze had sprung up, but it was steady and blowing across. I walked up to within about thirty-five paces of the two elephant and halted as one of them swung around, ears out and trunk up, and took a step or two towards me. He must have seen something moving but could not make out what it was. I waited for him to halt; shot him at the base of the throat; and then swung on his companion. By the time I was ready for him he was also facing me and I gave him an identical shot. Both elephant reacted in the same way: their hindquarters gave way and they squatted there for a few moments like two huge hogs whilst I reloaded. Then first one and then the other collapsed into the kneeling position and died like that. They both remained on their knees as you so often see elephant that have been brought down with frontal brain-shots.

Both these elephant had a number of old bullet-wounds. In fact every elephant I shot in here had been wounded in the past. But the wounds were all old—at least, if there were any fresh ones they must have been on the under side of those that fell flat. However, I do not think that many of them could have been hit recently, since there was very little ivory-hunting taking place at this time, except for my own operations. I knew that I had not wounded and lost an elephant for many years. We remained in here for some six or seven weeks and killed thirty-three elephant. It was certainly the easiest and pleasantest elephant-hunting I have ever enjoyed. Mostly the elephant were in pairs, although there were quite a number of lone bulls and several parties of three and four. No tusk ran below 50-lbs, while the average was well over 70-lbs, which is very good indeed.

Water was something of a problem at first, but we found several large baobabs with sufficient water in them to provide us all with occasional baths. And when you are not wearing clothes, you do not need to have a bath quite so often.